Pocket
PORTO

TOP SIGHTS • LOCAL LIFE • MADE EASY

Kerry Christiani

In This Book

QuickStart Guide

Your keys to understanding the city – we help you decide what to do and how to do it

Need to Know
Tips for a smooth trip

Neighbourhoods
What's where

Explore Porto

The best things to see and do, neighbourhood by neighbourhood

Top Sights
Make the most of your visit

Local Life
The insider's city

The Best of Porto

The city's highlights in handy lists to help you plan

Best Walks
See the city on foot

Porto's Best...
The best experiences

Survival Guide

Tips and tricks for a seamless, hassle-free city experience

Getting Around
Travel like a local

Essential Information
Including where to stay

Our selection of the city's best places to eat, drink and experience:

👁 **Sights**

✕ **Eating**

🍷 **Drinking**

⭐ **Entertainment**

🛍 **Shopping**

These symbols give you the vital information for each listing:

- 📞 Telephone Numbers
- 🕐 Opening Hours
- 🅿 Parking
- 🚭 Nonsmoking
- @ Internet Access
- 📶 Wi-Fi Access
- 🥗 Vegetarian Selection
- 📖 English-Language Menu
- 👨‍👩‍👧 Family-Friendly
- 🐾 Pet-Friendly
- 🚌 Bus
- ⛴ Ferry
- Ⓜ Metro
- Ⓢ Subway
- 🚊 Tram
- 🚆 Train

Find each listing quickly on maps for each neighbourhood:

Bar Hemingway

16 🍷 Map p233, B2

Legend has it that Hemi
self, wielding a machine
rate this timber-pan
ered bar during
showpiece is a
n by Papa ar
town. Dress
s.com; Hôtel Rit
; ⏰6.30pm-2a

Lonely Planet's Porto

Lonely Planet Pocket Guides are designed to get you straight to the heart of the city.

Inside you'll find all the must-see sights, plus tips to make your visit to each one really memorable. We've split the city into easy-to-navigate neighbourhoods and provided clear maps so you'll find your way around with ease. Our expert authors have searched out the best of the city: walks, food, nightlife and shopping, to name a few. Because you want to explore, our 'Local Life' pages will take you to some of the most exciting areas to experience the real Porto.

And of course you'll find all the practical tips you need for a smooth trip: itineraries for short visits, how to get around, and how much to tip the guy who serves you a drink at the end of a long day's exploration.

It's your guarantee of a really great experience.

Our Promise

You can trust our travel information because Lonely Planet authors visit the places we write about, each and every edition. We never accept freebies for positive coverage, so you can rely on us to tell it like it is.

The Best of Porto **123**

Porto's Best Walks

Porto's Best...

Survival Guide **143**

QuickStart Guide

Welcome to Porto

You can't always see the river in Porto, but you can feel it – running as smoothly as aged tawny being decanted in the port lodges marching grandly up its south bank. Hammered to the west by Atlantic waves, Porto entices with a pristine medieval centre, edgy architecture, high-spirited nightlife and a whole lot of soul. Trust us, you'll soon be smitten.

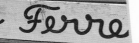

Barcos rabelos (traditional wooden boats used to transport wine)
ALAN COPSON/GETTY IMAGES ©

Porto
Top Sights

Sé (p24)

Gazing proudly over Porto from its hilltop perch, the fortress-like Sé evokes the city's past in its architecture and wields historical clout as the cathedral where Prince Henry the Navigator was baptised and King John I married.

Igreja de São Francisco (p26)

Dripping with gold leaf, this church's indulgent feast of baroque will bowl you over. Note the masterful Tree of Jesse in the nave and wander the eerie catacombs in contemplative silence.

Palácio da Bolsa
(p28)

Evoking the riches of
the past, no expense
was spared on the Stock
Exchange Palace's mosaic-
and mural-lined halls,
gorgeous swoop of a staircase and kaleidoscopic
Arabian Hall.

Museu Nacional Soares dos Reis
(p64)

A palatial repository for
Porto's standout fine and
decorative arts collection,
this museum heaves with
everything from the sen-
sual sculpture of António
Soares dos Reis to Dutch
painting and Chinese
porcelain.

Centro Português de Fotografia
(p66)

This former jailhouse
now rocks with exhib-
itions zooming in on
contemporary photogra-
phy and takes you back
to a sepia-hued age with
its collection of early-days
cameras.

Jardim do Palácio de Cristal (p96)

Peacocks parade around these botanical gardens spread lushly across the heights of Massarelos. The more you wander, the more you're drawn to hidden pockets of greenery where fountains burble and *miradouros* (lookouts) command dress-circle city views.

Casa da Música (p106)

Praise by critics exalts the acoustic wonders and architectural marvels of Porto's space-age concert hall, designed by Dutch daredevil Rem Koolhaas and home to the Porto National Orchestra.

Serralves (p120)

Out of the way but well worth the detour, Serralves brings together avant-garde architecture, cutting-edge art, a sculpture-strewn park and a bijou art-deco mansion in one harmonious whole.

Porto
Local Life

Insider tips to help you find the real city

Click into the city's unique groove by taking the lead of locals: dipping into quaint fishing villages and boho-cool neighbourhoods, peeling back the layers of Jewish heritage in cobbled backstreets and partying in retro-cool bars.

Galerias Bar Crawl (p44)

▶ Bar-hopping
▶ Late-night parties

Every inch the hipster party pen, Galerias has bumper-to-bumper bars made for crawling – from artsy-dowdy to vintage-chic, Parisian bordello to urbane sophisticate. Let the music and good vibes take you to nocturnal nirvana.

Jewish Porto (p68)

▶ Jewish heritage
▶ Old-world charm

Flick back to one of the most fascinating epochs in Porto's history with a mosey around this medieval warren of back-streets. You'll get an eye-opening sense of how Jewish life once thrived here, as well as snapshot city views from high-perched *miradouros* (lookouts).

Afurada (p92)

▶ Fish lunch (or supper)
▶ Riverfront walks

The lure of the sea is tangible in this speck of a village, reached by a little boat that splutters across the river. In a trend-obsessed world, Afurada is a restorative blast of go-slow nostalgia, with men hauling in the day's catch and women dishing the dirt at the public laundry.

Exploring Rua Miguel Bombarda (p98)

▶ Gallery-hopping
▶ Hipster hang-outs

Splashed with street art, Rua Miguel Bombarda is a new wave of galleries, boutiques, vintage shops and concept stores bringing fledgling designers and fresh-faced Porto creatives to the fore.

Foz do Douro (p116)

▶ Beach walks
▶ Fine dining

Out west, Foz do Douro lures locals and travellers with beach bars and excellent restaurants. Walk the seafront esplanade, thrashed by Atlantic waves, or just kick back on the beach.

Ar de Rio (p86)

Mercado do Bolhão (p61)

Other great places to experience the city like a local:

ViniPortugal (p38)

Taste Porto Food Tours (p51)

Casa do Evaristo (p52)

Mercado do Bolhão (p61)

Almada 13 (p48)

Rua São Pedro de Miragaia (p72)

Ar de Rio (p86)

Igreja do Corpo Santo de Massarelos (p101)

Mercado Bom Sucesso (p110)

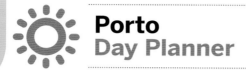

Porto
Day Planner

Day One

☀ Begin where the city itself began in Ribeira: a charismatic tangle of alleyways and chalk-hued houses toppling haphazardly down the hillside. These lanes are packed with historical anecdotes and crowd-pulling sights. First up is the **Igreja de São Francisco** (p26), which packs a glitzy punch with its baroque excess. Make a beeline for the star attraction Tree of Jesse before delving down to the catacombs, echoing with ghosts of Porto past.

☀ Lunch on the terrace of deli **Mercearia das Flores** (p34) before a shop along pretty Rua das Flores – pop into **Chocolateria Ecuador** (p40) for chocs and **Tradições** (p40) for real-deal souvenirs. Ambling south brings you to the stoutly neoclassical **Palácio da Bolsa** (Stock Exchange Palace; p28), with interiors shimmering with chandeliers, skylit murals and Moorish-style artistry – a whirlwind guided tour breezes through them.

☽ As day melts into watercolour dusk, **Cais da Ribeira** (p32) hums with the life of market stalls, street entertainers and pavement cafes – all framed by the graceful swoop of **Ponte de Dom Luís I** (p32). After pre-dinner drinks and appetisers at **Wine Quay Bar** (p38), bag a riverfront table at **Casinha São João** (p35) for Portuguese-style tapas prepared with flair.

Day Two

☀ Start your morning by exploring the handsome fin-de-siècle **São Bento train station** (p48), recounting Porto's history in *azulejos* (hand-painted tiles). From here, the beguiling **Avenida dos Aliados** (p48) unfurls north with beaux-arts-style swagger. Duck down a backstreet to reach **Mercado do Bolhão** (p61), a 19th-century market hall brimming with fresh produce and local banter.

☀ Refuel over a light lunch at opulent **Café Majestic** (p126) or a classic *francesinha* (open roast meat, ham and sausage sandwich topped with melted cheese, a fried egg and beer sauce) at **Cafe Santiago** (p54). Sated, backtrack to the **Sé** (p24) for a culture fix and cracking city views. That bridge you keep seeing? Now it's time to walk across it to reach the hilltop **Jardim do Morro** (p83) for more precipitous views. Zip down to Vila Nova de Gaia's waterfront in the cable car, then hit one of the port-wine lodges for a cellar tour and tasting – **Taylor's** (p84) is hard to beat.

☽ Back in the heart of town, go for dinner at charismatic **Flor dos Congregados** (p51), which champions regional field-to-fork grub, then check out the bars as the mood, music and drinks take you in the **Galerias** (p44).

Short on time?

We've arranged Porto's must-sees into these day-by-day itineraries to make sure you see the very best of the city in the time you have available.

Day Three

☀ Start sweetly over feather-light éclairs and a *cimbalinho* (espresso) at **Leitaria Quinta Do Paço** (p50) before soaking up Miragaia's sights. Photography buffs won't want to miss jail-turned-gallery **Centro Português de Fotografia** (p66). Allow time to saunter the former Jewish quarter at leisure, where historic surprises and above-the-rooftop views await.

☀ Immerse yourself in local life over lunch at down-to-earth **Taberna de Santo António** (p69), then cut north through the **Jardim da Cordoaria** (p72) to the **Museu Nacional Soares dos Reis** (p64) – a major drawcard for anyone into fine and decorative arts. One street over is **Rua Miguel Bombarda** (p98), ideal for a mooch with its kooky boutiques and up-to-the-minute galleries. Stop for a fragrant cuppa at delightfully boho **Rota do Chá** (p99), then wind out the afternoon in the botanical tranquillity of **Jardim do Palácio de Cristal** (p96).

☽ Take your pick – either go for a rooftop dinner with city views followed by a concert at the iconic **Casa da Música** (p106) or head back into town. It's your penultimate night in Porto, so all the more reason to celebrate by booking a top table like **DOP** (p36) or **Cantinho do Avillez** (p35).

Day Four

☀ Four days in Porto gives you time to tiptoe off the tourist trail west. Browse the latest contemporary art exhibition at the **Museu de Arte Contemporânea** (p121), dawdling to explore its lake-speckled gardens and art-deco mansion. From here, edge west to the seaside **Foz do Douro** (p116), a soothing tonic to the buzz of the city.

☀ Grab a bite to eat at **Tavi** (p117), a Foz stalwart famous for its patisserie and ice cream. Wander along the ocean-front promenade, where the crash of Atlantic waves soothes and reawakens the senses, or go for a paddle off one of the rocky beaches. If you've kids in tow, **Sealife Porto** (p117) beckons with its marine-life oddities.

☽ If you fancy staying beachside while the Atlantic dips below the horizon, make your way to **Praia da Luz** (p118) for a sundowner. What better way to end your Porto break than dinner at the **Boa Nova Tea House** (p118) – the combined effort of starchitect Álvaro Siza Vieira and chef Rui Paula. Eat sublimely prepared seafood as tides batter the rocks outside.

Need to Know

For more information, see Survival Guide (p143)

Currency
Euro (€)

Language
Portuguese

Visas
EU nationals need no visa. US, Canadian, Australian and New Zealand visitors can stay for up to 90 days without a visa.

Money
ATMs widely available. Credit cards generally accepted, but cash preferred in some small shops and restaurants. Ask first.

Mobile Phones
Portugal uses the GSM 900/1800 frequency. European and Australian mobile phones work. US travellers should check with their service provider. Save on roaming charges by investing in a local SIM card.

Time
Porto is on GMT/UTC.

Plugs & Adaptors
Plugs have two round pins; electrical current is 220V. North American and US visitors will need an adaptor.

Tipping
Service is not usually added to the bill. Tip an average of 10% if you are satisfied with the service.

① Before You Go

Your Daily Budget

Budget less than €60
► Dorm bed €18–22
► Lunch specials and fixed-price menus
► Sightseeing on free admission days (usually Sunday morning); free city tours

Midrange €60–150
► Double room in a central hotel €50–120
► Meal in a midrange restaurant €20–30
► Guided half-day bike tour from €15; tour of a port cellar including tasting €5

Top end more than €150
► Boutique double from €100
► Three-course dinner with wine from €40
► Theatre/concert tickets €15–30; full-day tour of the Rio Douro €90

Useful Websites

Lonely Planet (www.lonelyplanet.com/portugal/the-north/porto) Destination information, hotel bookings, traveller forum and more.

Visit Porto (www.visitporto.travel) Official tourist office website.

O Porto Cool (www.oportocool.wordpress.com) Keep tabs on what's cool.

Spotted by Locals (www.spottedbylocals.com/porto) Inside scoop from locals.

Advance Planning

One month before Book hotel rooms, festival, theatre and concert tickets, excursions.

Two weeks before Reserve a table at the city's top restaurants.

A few days before Check what's happening on events websites. Learn about port wine – www.taylor.pt gives an overview.

2 Arriving in Porto

Most visitors arrive at Porto's Francisco Sá Carneiro Airport (www.ana.pt), 17km north-west of the city centre. Metro connections to the centre run frequently. Line E (the violet one) runs every 20 to 30 minutes from 6am to 12.30am; single tickets cost €1.85. Taxis depart in front of arrivals and charge €20 to €30 for the ride to central Porto.

✈ From Francisco Sá Carneiro Airport

Destination	Best Transport
Aliados	Metro line E (direction Estádio do Dragão) to Trindade, change to line D (direction Santo Ovídio)
São Bento	Metro line E (direction Estádio do Dragão) to Trindade, change to line D (direction Santo Ovídio)
Bolhão	Metro line E (direction Estádio do Dragão)
Cordoaria	Bus 601

✈ At the Airport

Porto's gleaming Francisco Sá Carneiro Airport is modern and easy to navigate. It has numerous cafes, bars, restaurants and shops, as well as a post office, ATMs, baby-changing facilities, car rental, and left luggage and a tourist information. The first 30 minutes of wi-fi is free for passengers.

3 Getting Around

Public transport is inexpensive and efficient. Save time and money by investing in a 24-hour pass (€7), covering the entire network except for trams. For timetables, routes and fares, see www.stcp.pt and www.metrodo-porto.pt.

M Metro

Porto's compact, six-line metro network runs from 6am to 1am daily. It's handy for zipping between neighbourhoods and getting to/from the airport and beaches north of the city. A map is available at www.metrodoporto.pt. Single tickets for central zones cost €1.20 with a chargeable Andante Card (€0.60).

🚋 Tram

Porto's vintage trams are transport at its atmospheric best. There are three lines: 1E running along the river from the historic centre to Foz; 18 between Massarelos and Carmo; and 22 doing a loop through the centre from Carmo to Batalha/Guindais. Single tickets cost €2.50, day passes €8.

🚌 Bus

Central hubs of Porto's extensive bus system include the Jardim da Cordoaria, Praça da Liberdade and São Bento station. Tickets purchased on the bus are one-way; €1.20/€1.85 with/without the Andante Card.

🚗 Taxi

To cross town, expect to pay between €5 and €8. There's a 20% surcharge at night. There are taxi ranks throughout the centre or call ☎ 225 076 400.

Porto
Neighbourhoods

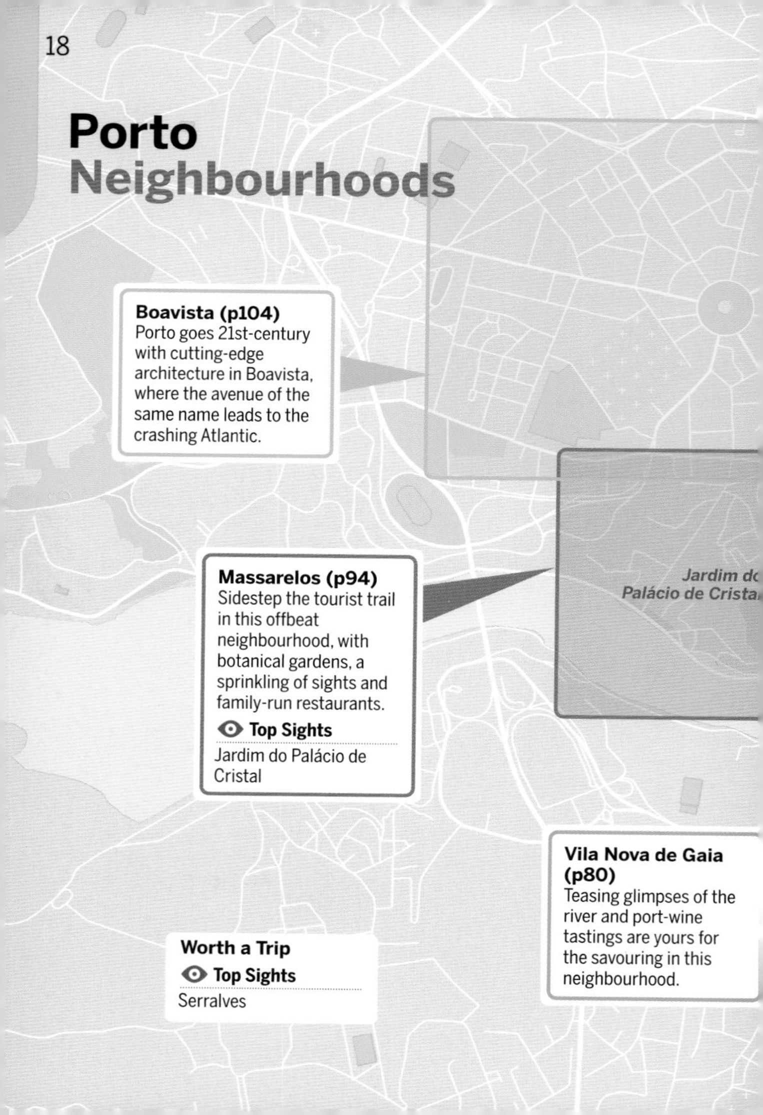

Boavista (p104)
Porto goes 21st-century with cutting-edge architecture in Boavista, where the avenue of the same name leads to the crashing Atlantic.

Massarelos (p94)
Sidestep the tourist trail in this offbeat neighbourhood, with botanical gardens, a sprinkling of sights and family-run restaurants.

◉ Top Sights

Jardim do Palácio de Cristal

Jardim do
Palácio de Cristal

Vila Nova de Gaia (p80)
Teasing glimpses of the river and port-wine tastings are yours for the savouring in this neighbourhood.

Worth a Trip
◉ Top Sights

Serralves

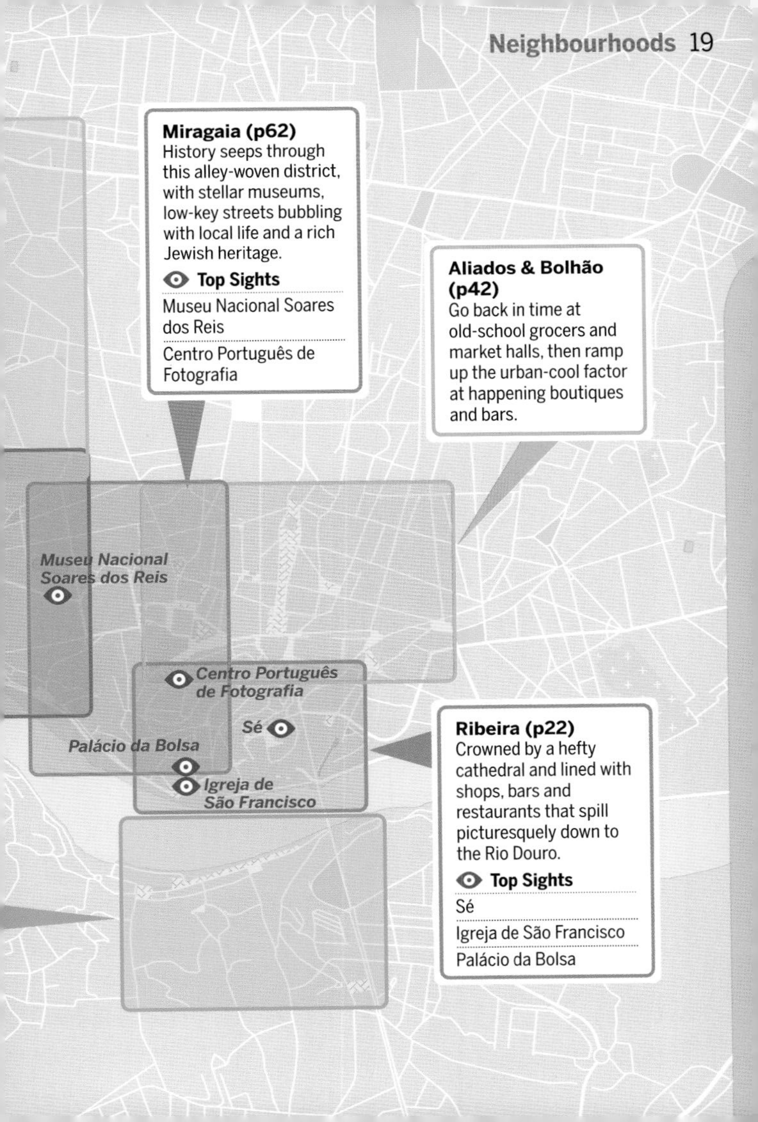

Miragaia (p62)

History seeps through this alley-woven district, with stellar museums, low-key streets bubbling with local life and a rich Jewish heritage.

⊙ Top Sights

Museu Nacional Soares dos Reis

Centro Português de Fotografia

Aliados & Bolhão (p42)

Go back in time at old-school grocers and market halls, then ramp up the urban-cool factor at happening boutiques and bars.

Museu Nacional Soares dos Reis
⊙

Centro Português de Fotografia ⊙

Sé ⊙

Palácio da Bolsa

⊙ *Igreja de São Francisco*

Ribeira (p22)

Crowned by a hefty cathedral and lined with shops, bars and restaurants that spill picturesquely down to the Rio Douro.

⊙ Top Sights

Sé

Igreja de São Francisco

Palácio da Bolsa

Explore
Porto

Worth a Trip

Ponte de Dom Luís I (p32)
MAREMAGNUM/GETTY IMAGES ©

Explore

Ribeira

Ribeira is Porto's biggest heart-stealer. Its Unesco World Heritage maze of medieval alleys zigzags down to the Rio Douro and a promenade lined with slender, pastel-hued houses and hole-in-the-wall *tascas* (taverns) with front-row views of the spectacular Ponte de Dom Luís I. Jam-packed with sights, shops and restaurants, this historic neighbourhood is postcard Porto.

The Sights in a Day

☼ Begin at the Romanesque **Sé** (p24), Porto's fortified Roman- esque cathedral, which lords it over the city and affords ravishing views over the rooftops from its terrace. From here, meander deep into the medieval alleys of the Unesco World Heritage historic centre. Particularly pretty is **Rua das Flores**, which rambles past tiled houses with Juliet balconies, the beautiful *azulejo*-clad **Igreja da Misericórdia** (p32), enticing pavement cafes and speciality shops.

☼ Stop for an organic lunch or a cup of Azores tea at rustic deli **Mercearia das Flores** (p34). Recharged, join a guided tour at the lavish **Palácio da Bolsa** (p28), where a grand staircase curls up to the kaleido- scopically intricate Arabian Hall. Take a breather in the **Jardim do Infante D Henrique** (p32) before turning the corner to the **Igreja de São Francisco** (p26), which bombards you with its gilded baroque splendour.

☾ As day softens into golden dusk, amble to **Cais da Ribeira** (p32), where the hum of chatter drifts from cafes, *tascas* and market stalls, buskers entertain crowds and the iconic **Ponte de Dom Luís I** (p32) straddles the Douro. Watch the port lodges on the opposite bank light up one by one over pre-dinner drinks at **Wine Quay Bar** (p38).

◎ Top Sights

Sé (p24)

Igreja de São Francisco (p26)

Palácio da Bolsa (p28)

♥ Best of Porto

Eating

Bacalhau (p35)

Cantinho do Avillez (p35)

DOP (p36)

Ode Porto Wine House (p37)

Nightlife & Entertainment

Vinologia (p37)

Prova (p38)

Hot Five Jazz & Blues Club (p40)

Shopping

Chocolateria Ecuador (p40)

Tradições (p40)

Getting There

Ⓜ **Metro** São Bento (yellow metro line D).

🚊 **Tram** Tram 1 runs along the river, linking the historic centre to Passeio Alegre in Foz. It stops on Rua Nova da Alfândega in front of the Igreja de São Francisco.

Top Sights
Sé

Rising high and mighty above Porto's tangle of medieval alleys and stairways, this hulking, hilltop fortress of a cathedral was founded in the 12th century, rebuilt a century later and given a baroque makeover in the 18th century. History, however, lends it gravitas – this is where Prince Henry the Navigator was baptised in 1394, the fortune of far-flung lands but a distant dream, and where King John I married his beloved Philippa of Lancaster in 1387.

⊙ Map p30, F3

Terreiro da Sé

cloisters adult/student €3/2

⊙ 9am-12.30pm & 2.30-7pm Apr-Oct, to 6pm Nov-Mar

Don't Miss

Facade

Located strategically on a hillside, the cathedral is visible from afar. The terrace grants sweeping views that reach over the historic centre's lanes and rooftops and down to the Douro. Carved from local granite, the facade resembles a fortress with its pair of sturdy towers and crenellations. You can still make out its Romanesque contours.

Interior

The Romanesque barrel-vaulted nave and the Gothic rose window recall the cathedral's earlier origins. Keep an eye out for the baroque altarpiece in the Chapel of the Holy Sacrament, exquisitely wrought from silver, the Gothic funerary chapel of João Gordo, a Knight Hospitaller for King Dinis I, and Portuguese sculptor António Teixeira Lopes' bronze bas-relief depicting Christ's baptism by John the Baptist.

Cloister & Loggia

Blue and white *azulejos* (hand-painted tiles) dating from the 18th century and evoking scenes from the Song of Solomon dance elegantly across the walls of the Gothic cloister, a peaceful spot for a contemplative stroll. The baroque loggia by Italian architect Nicolau Nasoni is adorned with more beautiful 18th-century tiles by Valentim de Almeida, which show the life of the Virgin Mary.

Courtyards

There are several treasures in the cathedral courtyards. Look out for a barley-twist neo-Pombaline pillary and the Chafariz de São Miguel, an 18th-century fountain by Nasoni topped with a little statue of St Michael the Archangel. In the grounds, notice too the grand baroque facade of the Paço Episcopal, former residence of the bishops of Porto.

☑ Top Tips

▶ Come back to the cathedral as day softens into dusk for photogenic views of the Old Town and river.

▶ Dip into the maze of surrounding alleyways for a serendipitous wander.

▶ To truly feel the spirit of the cathedral, attend one of the services – 11am mass on Sunday and 7pm evensong daily.

✖ Take a Break

Sweeten your day with cupcakes, tarts, brownies and dreamily smooth gelato at nearby **Spirito** (Map p30, E1; Rua Mouzinho da Silveira 324; sweets & ice cream €2-4; ⏱1.30-7pm Mon & Tue, 1.30-7pm & 9pm-midnight Wed-Sat).

Mercearia das Flores (p34) is a delightful deli just a five-minute toddle away. The food is healthy and mostly organic and there is pavement seating.

Top Sights
Igreja de São Francisco

How deceptive appearances can be. Sitting plump on Praça Infante Dom Henrique, the Igreja de São Francisco looks for all the world like an austerely Gothic church from the outside, but inside it hides one of Portugal's most dazzling displays of baroque finery. Hardly an inch escapes unsmothered, as otherworldly cherubs and sober monks are drowned by nearly 100kg of gold leaf – shimmering with light from the rose window. If you only see one church in Porto, make it this one.

👁 Map p30, B4

Praça Infante Dom Henrique

adult/child €3.50/1.75

🕐 9am-8pm Jul-Sep, to 7pm Mar-Jun & Oct, to 6pm Nov-Feb

Don't Miss

The Nave

This golden wonder bombards you with exuberant ornament. Interwoven with vines and curlicues, dripping with cherubs and shot through with gold, its carved vaults and pillars elicit gasps of incredulity from visitors. Peel back the layers of detail to find standouts like the Manueline-style Chapel of St John the Baptist and the 13th-century granite statue of St Francis of Assisi.

Tree of Jesse

The handiwork of master craftsmen Filipe da Silva and António Gomes, this polychrome marvel of an altarpiece (1718 and 1721) traces the genealogy of Christ. The tree roots grow from the loins of a reclining Jesse of Bethlehem at the base up into branches with the 12 kings of Judah. In a niche is the Virgin Mary and infant Jesus.

Church Museum

Opposite the church, the museum harbours a fine, well-edited collection of sacred art. Besides portraits of bishops in all their ecclesiastical finery, there are some beautiful baroque altarpieces, tabernacles, silverware and ceramics. On the ground floor of the museum, one of the star pieces is a 1799 painting of St Louis, King of France, by famous Porto-born artist Vieira Portuense.

Catacombs

In the eerily atmospheric catacombs, the great and the good of Porto were once buried; in fact, all Portuguese were buried in churches before 1845 as public cemeteries did not exist. Tiptoe past the headstones, looking out for sculptural works by Italian master Nicolau Nasoni and prolific Portuguese sculptor António Teixeira Lopes. The ossuary is a spine-tingling work of art.

☑ Top Tips

▶ Tram 1 stops right in front of the church. Hop aboard it and you can be beside the sea in Foz do Douro within minutes.

▶ Leave digicams and smartphones behind – photography is not permitted.

▶ To see the church at its quiet best, rise early to be there as it opens, or come in early evening in summer.

✕ Take a Break

Try to bag a table on the terrace at nearby Bacalhau (p35) for cracking river views as you chomp on *petiscos* (tapas) or creative takes on codfish.

For traditional Portuguese grub, mooch over to A Grade (p36), where the seafood is super-fresh and the welcome warm.

Top Sights
Palácio da Bolsa

One glimpse at the lavish interiors of Porto's Palácio da Bolsa tells you precisely who once held the purse strings. Built from 1842 to 1910, this splendid neoclassical monument honours Porto's past and present money merchants. Dressed to impress, its halls are replete with exquisite murals, mosaics and artworks. It's a fittingly grand backdrop for hosting visiting heads of state, and the Sala do Tribunal is the setting for the momentous occasion when port is declared vintage.

Stock Exchange Palace

👁 Map p30, B4

Rua Ferreira Borges

tours adult/child €7/4

🕑 9am-6.30pm Apr-Oct, 9am-12.30pm & 2-5.30pm Nov-Mar

Don't Miss

Salão Árabe

The palace's crowning glory is the stupendous Arabian Hall, with stucco teased into complex Moorish designs, then gilded with some 20kg of gold. Inspired by the Alhambra, it has arabesques dancing across its polychrome walls and columns rising gracefully to keyhole arches and stained-glass windows. No surface is left untouched.

Pátio das Nações

The Hall of Nations is the first thing you see as you enter – and it's a stunner. Lit by an octagonal skylight, this courtyard is where the exchange operated. You'll see the coat of arms of Portugal and the countries with which it once traded, and the Greco-Roman floor mosaic inspired by Pompeii.

Gabinete de Gustave Eiffel

This simply furnished study is where that famous French civil engineer architect Gustave Eiffel beavered away from 1875 to 1877, the Eiffel Tower then but a Parisian twinkle in his eye. The study has a view of the Ponte de Dom Luís I, but it is the Ponte Maria Pia, just out of sight, that bears his hallmark.

Escadaria Noble

Beautifully wrought in granite, the Noble Staircase took 68 years to complete because it was so hard to carve. Look for the busts of feted sculptors António Soares dos Reis and António Teixeira Lopes, a pair of striking bronze chandeliers and the ceiling frescoes by António Ramalho.

Sala do Tribunal

You can feel the weight of history in this grand courtroom, with its ornately carved wooden benches and vivid murals showing the wealth of commercial activity in the city and region. To this day, this is where port is declared 'vintage'.

☑ Top Tips

▶ To visit the interior, you'll need to hook onto one of the half-hour guided tours, which set off every 30 minutes.

▶ In the Sala dos Retratos (Portrait Hall), take a peek at the intricate table, which took engraver Zeferino José Pinto three years to carve with a pocket knife.

✗ Take a Break

Linger in the splendour of the palace over lunch or dinner at O Comercial (p36), which serves Mediterranean flavours with a touch of class.

Only fancy a quick bite to eat? Pop around the corner to Porto Bagel Cafe (p35) which rustles up good bagels, salads and coffee.

N

0 ——————— 180 m
0 ——————— 0.1 miles

R das Flo

R das Taipas

R S Bento da Vitória

R da Vitória

11

R São Miguel

R Mouzinho da Silve

R Virtudes

Igreja da
Misericórdia 5
9 Museu das
Marionetas
21
16
R da Bainha

20

R de Belmonte

12
Largo de
São Domingos

38
22
R Sousa Viterbo

29

25

R Santana

Largo de
São João
Novo 28

R São João Novo

Instituto dos Vinhos
do Douro e do Porto 6

32

R Ferreira Borges

19

R de São João

R dos Mercadores

R da Bolsa

Praça Infante
Dom Henrique

27

24

R do Comércio do Porto

Palácio
da Bolsa

Jardim do
Infante D
Henrique 1

R R São Francisco

17

R Nova da Alfândega

Igreja de São
Francisco

R Infante Dom Henrique

Casa do
Infante 8

Praça
Ríbei

14

2

R São Nicolau

36
33

R Alfândega

iPoir
Ribeir

18

37

23
26

R de Fonte Taurina

R da Reboleira

Largo do
Terreiro

R Outeirinho

15

Muro dos Bacalhoeiros

E

34 🔒

🔒 **35**

São Bento Ⓜ F

G

H

R dos Pelames

R do Loureiro

R do Cimo de Vila

R do Cativo

Av Dom Afonso Henriques

R Chã

R Portas do Sol

R Augusto Rosa

1

2

R Saraiva Carvalho

Largo 1 de Dezembro

🔲

◉ **Sé**

Terreiro da Sé

ℹ Turismo (Sé)

Av Vimara Peres

7 ◉

Igreja de Santa Clara

R Arnaldo Gama

☆ **30**

3

R de Dom Hugo

R S Verdades

R Miradouro

10 ◉▸

4

R Barredo

Funicular dos Guindais

Av Gustavo Eiffel

s Baixo

R Canastreiros

Cais da Ribeira

R de Cima do Muro

Cais da Ribeira

✖ **13**

◉ **3**

Rio Douro

Ponte de **4** ◉ Dom Luís I

5

Sights

Jardim do Infante D Henrique

GARDENS, PLAZA

1 ◉ Map p30, C4

Presided over by the late-19th-century market hall Mercado Ferreira Borges and neoclassical Palácio da Bolsa, this plaza is named after its centrepiece statue. Lifted high on a pedestal is great navigator Prince Henry the Navigator (1394–1460), a catalyst in the Age of Discovery and pioneer of the caravel, who braved the battering Atlantic in search of colonies for Portugal's collection. (Rua Ferreira Borges)

Understand
A Bridge Over the Douro's Troubled Waters

- - - - - - - - - - - - - - -

The construction of the Ponte de Dom Luís I was significant, as the area's foot traffic once travelled across a bridge made from old port boats lashed together. To make matters worse, the river was wild back then, with no upstream dams. When Napoleon invaded in 1809, scores were crushed and drowned in the rushing river as a panicked stampede proved too much for the makeshift bridge.

When the bridge was completed in 1886 by German architect Téophile Seyrig, who Gustave Eiffel had taken under his wing, it held the record for the longest iron arch in the world, with a span of 172m.

Praça da Ribeira

PLAZA

2 ◉ Map p30, D5

Down by the river, narrow streets open out onto a plaza framed by austerely grand, tiled townhouses overlooking a picturesque stretch of the Rio Douro. From here you have fine views of the port-wine lodges across the river as well as the monumental, double-decker Ponte de Dom Luís I.

Cais da Ribeira

QUAY

3 ◉ Map p30, F5

This riverfront promenade takes in the whole spectacular sweep of the city – from Ribeira's skinny pastel houses to the *barcos rabelos* (flat-bottomed boats) once used to transport port from the Douro. Buskers serenade crowds and chefs fire up grills in the hole-in-the-wall fish restaurants and *tascas* (taverns) in the old arcades.

Ponte de Dom Luís I

BRIDGE

4 ◉ Map p30, G5

Completed in 1886 by a student of Gustave Eiffel, the bridge's top deck is now reserved for pedestrians, as well as one of the city's metro lines; the lower deck bears regular traffic, with narrow pedestrian walkways lining the road. The views of the river and Old Town are simply stunning.

Igreja da Misericórdia

CHURCH

5 ◉ Map p30, C2

Discreetly hidden behind a wrought-iron grille, you'll find the rococo

Igreja de Santa Clara

facade of this 16th-century church designed by the Italian baroque architect Nicolau Nasoni. The interior is adorned with beautiful blue and white *azulejos* (hand-painted tiles). Closed at the time of research for renovation, the church museum boasts a superb Renaissance painting, *Fons Vitae* (Fountain of Life). (Rua das Flores 5; ☉8am-noon & 2-5.30pm Tue-Fri, 8.30am-12.30pm Sat & Sun)

Instituto dos Vinhos do Douro e do Porto   NOTABLE BUILDING

6 ◉ Map p30, C3

When area vintners apply for the certification that ultimately christens their casks with the term 'Port', they bring vials to the labs set in this attractive relic just uphill from the river. The labs are off-limits to visitors, but you're welcome to explore the lobby exhibits, and the attached wine shop offers tastings. (www.ivdp.pt; Rua Ferreira Borges 27; wine tasting €5; ☉11am-7pm Mon-Fri)

Igreja de Santa Clara   CHURCH

7 ◉ Map p30, G3

Once part of a Franciscan convent, this church hides an opulent interior behind its unassuming facade. Gothic in shape, with a fine Renaissance portal, its baroque interior is dense with elaborately gilded woodwork. (Largo 1 de Dezembro; ☉9.30am-noon & 3.30-7pm Mon-Fri, 10am-noon & 3-6pm Sat, 10am-noon Sun)

Casa do Infante　HISTORIC BUILDING

8　　Map p30, C4

Just back from the river is this handsomely renovated medieval townhouse where, according to legend, Henry the Navigator was born in 1394. The building later served as Porto's first customs house. Today it houses three floors of exhibits. In 2002 the complex was excavated, revealing Roman foundations and some remarkable mosaics – all of which are now on display. (Rua Alfândega 10; adult/child €2.20/free; ⏲9.30am-1pm & 2-5.30pm Tue-Sun)

Museu das Marionetas　MUSEUM

9　　Map p30, C2

Porto's marionette museum turns the spotlight on the remarkable puppet creations that have taken to the stage at the Teatro Marionetas do Porto over the past 25 years. Rotating exhibitions present marionettes from productions like *Macbeth* and *Cinderella*. (www.marionetasdoporto.pt; Rua das Flores 22; admission €2; ⏲11am-1pm & 2-6pm Mon-Sat; 👶)

Ponte Maria Pia　BRIDGE

10　　Map p30, H4

The Ponte de Dom Luís I might hog the limelight, but it is this railway bridge, slightly further east, that bears the hallmark of Gustave Eiffel. Built when the Eiffel Tower was but a twinkle in his eye, the bridge was a remarkable feat of engineering and the longest single-arch span in the world when it was completed in 1877.

Eating

Mercearia das Flores　DELI €

11　　Map p30, D2

This rustic-chic delicatessen food store serves all-day *petiscos* (tapas) made with organic regional products on the three tables and two counters of its bright and airy interior. You can also order wines by the glass, tea from the Azores and locally brewed Sovina beer. Try the spicy sardines and salad on dark, sweet *broa* (cornbread). (Rua das Flores 110; petiscos €2.50-5.50; ⏲10am-7.30pm Mon-Thu, 10am-9pm Fri & Sat, 1-7pm Sun)

Top Tip

Six Bridges Cruise

A relaxed way to experience Porto on a fine day is from the deck of one of **Douro Azul's** (☎223 402 500; www.douroazul.com; 6 bridges cruise adult/child €10/5; ⏲9.30am-6.30pm) colourful ersatz *barcos rabelos* (flat-bottomed boats) that ply the river. The sights of Ribeira and Vila Nova de Gaia drift into view on the highly scenic tours, which last around 50 minutes and depart from Cais de Ribeira.

Taberna do Largo

PORTUGUESE €

12 🍴 Map p30, C3

Lit by wine-bottle lights, this sweet grocery store, deli and tavern is run with passion by Joana and Sofia. Tour Portugal with your tastebuds with their superb array of hand-picked wines, which go brilliantly with tasting platters of smoked tuna, Alentejo *salpicão* (sausage), Azores São Jorge cheese, Beira *morcela* (black sausage), *tremoços* (lupin beans) and more. (📞222 082 154; Largo de São Domingos 69; tapas €2-14; ⏰5pm-midnight Tue-Thu, 5pm-1am Fri, noon-1am Sat, noon-1am Sun)

Casinha São João

PORTUGUESE €

13 🍴 Map p30, E5

With tables gathered under stone arches and big river views from the terrace, this is a truly charming place for drinks and tapas. The welcome is warm and the kitchen serves simple and tasty dishes that are perfect for sharing – from grilled prawns to *feijoada* (bean stew) and *rojões* (strips of seasoned pork loin). (📞914 237 742, 220 197 889; http://casinhasaojoao.com; Cais da Ribeira 9; tapas €3.50-7; ⏰noon-midnight Tue-Sun)

Porto Bagel Cafe

SNACKS €

14 🍴 Map p30, A5

A bright, chipper choice down by the river, this cafe rustles up pretty decent breakfasts, bagels, fresh salads and daily specials (€7.50). Or stop by for

coffee and cake. (📞222 011 274; Rua Nova da Alfândega 12; bagels €5-7; ⏰8am-10pm; 🛜♿)

Bacalhau

PORTUGUESE €€

15 🍴 Map p30, B5

The name *bacalhau* (codfish) should give you an inkling as to the star of the menu at this slick riverside restaurant. Snag a terrace table to watch the boats chug by while digging into all-Portuguese petiscos (tapas) and delicious bacalhau-inspired dishes with creative edge, ranging from fresh cod with tomato puree and asparagus to codfish gratin with chestnuts and spinach. (📞960 378 883; http://bacalhauporto.com; Muro dos Bacalhoeiros 153; petiscos €3-8.50, mains €9-16; ⏰noon-11pm Sun-Thu, noon-11.45pm Fri & Sat)

Cantinho do Avillez

GOURMET €€

16 🍴 Map p30, D2

Star chef José Avillez' latest venture is a welcome newcomer to Porto's gastro scene. A bright, contemporary bistro with a retro spin, the Cantinho keeps the mood casual and buzzy. On the menu are seasonal Portuguese dishes with a pinch of creativity – from sautéed poultry liver with port marmalade to Alentejo black pork with French fries, coriander and garlic. (📞223 227 879; http://cantinhodoavillez. pt; Rua Mouzinho da Silveira 166; mains €17-39.50; ⏰12.30-3pm & 7pm-midnight Mon-Fri, 12.30pm-midnight Sat & Sun)

O Comercial
MODERN EUROPEAN €€

17 🍴 Map p30, B4

A touch of class in the Palácio da Bolsa, O Comercial has a whiff of romantic grandeur with its chandeliers, high ceilings and *azulejo*-clad walls. The service is polished and the menu places the accent on well-prepared Med-style classics, such as veal carpaccio with pesto, and tuna steak with port wine and onion sauce. (☏918 838 649; www.ocomercial.com; Palácio da Bolsa, Rua Ferreira Borges; 3-course dinner set menu €25; ⏱12.30-3pm & 7.30-10.30pm Mon-Fri, 7.30-11.30pm Sat)

A Grade
PORTUGUESE €€

18 🍴 Map p30, C5

Both a humble mum-and-dad operation and a masterwork of traditional fare, with generously portioned standouts such as baked octopus in butter and wine, and grilled seafood casseroles. Reservations recommended. (☏223 321 130; Rua da São Nicolau 9; mains €9-17.50; ⏱12.30-4pm & 6.30-11pm; 🍴)

O Mercado
INTERNATIONAL €€

19 🍴 Map p30, C4

On the top level of this born-again, late-19th-century market hall, O Mercado is a highly atmospheric pick, with its soaring ceiling, recycled palette tables and oil-barrel chairs. The crowd is youngish and the menu has an international slant, swinging from a light prawn and sundried tomato linguine to sirloin steak. (☏935 274 536; Mercado Ferreira Borges, Praça Infante Dom Henrique; light bites & snacks €5.50-12.50, mains €17-28; ⏱12.30pm-3am; 🚶)

LSD
MODERN EUROPEAN €€

20 🍴 Map p30, C2

Nothing to do with mind-bending drugs as its name suggests, this slick, contemporary bistro sets the scene with soft lighting and lemon and grey hues. The chef cooks clean, bright flavours with a pinch of creativity, be it free-range chicken served with nectarines or watermelon ice cream with pennyroyal ice cream. There's always a good buzz. (☏223 231 268; Largo de São Domingos 78; mains €10-18; ⏱10am-11pm Mon-Thu, 10am-midnight Fri & Sat)

Cantina 32
TAPAS €€

21 🍴 Map p30, C2

Industrial-chic meets boho at this delightfully laid-back haunt, with its walls of polished concrete, mismatched crockery, plants and vintage knick-knacks from a bicycle to an old typewriter. The menu is just as informal – *petiscos* like pica-pau steak, quail egg croquettes and cheesecake served in a flower pot reveal a pinch of creativity. (☏222 039 069; www.cantina32.com; Rua das Flores 32; petiscos €5-15; ⏱12.30-2.30pm & 7.30-11pm)

DOP
PORTUGUESE €€€

22 🍴 Map p30, C3

Housed in the Palácio das Artes, DOP is one of Porto's most stylish ad-

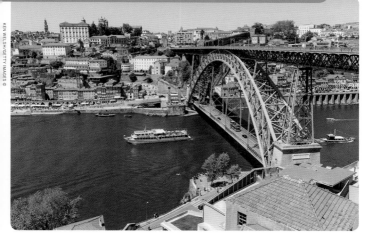

Ponte de Dom Luís I (p32)

dresses, with its high ceilings and slick, monochrome interior. Much-feted chef Rui Paula puts a creative, seasonal twist on outstanding ingredients. The eight-course tasting menu is the way to go, with delicate, flavour-packed dishes skipping from octopus carpaccio to cod with lobster rice. (☑222 014 313; www.ruipaula.com; Largo de São Domingos 18; tasting menu €65; ☺7-11pm Mon, 12.30-3pm & 7-11pm Tue-Sat)

Ode Porto Wine House

PORTUGUESE €€€

23 Map p30, C5

A slow-food hideaway just up from the Ribeira, with chestnut wood beams, exposed stone walls and slate tables

on wine barrels. The ingredients are all Portuguese – bread from Bragança, oregano from Algarve, smoked pork from Minho and sheep's cheese from Alentejo – and the dishes have a story. Reservations required. (☑913 200 010; Largo do Terreiro 7; mains €16-21; ☺7-11pm Tue-Sun)

Drinking

Vinologia

WINE BAR

24 🍷 Map p30, D4

This cosy wine bar is an excellent place to sample the fine quaffs of Porto, with over 200 different ports on offer. If you fall in love with a certain

Local Life
Wine Tasting Porto-Style

Housed in the grand Palácio da Bolsa, the **ViniPortugal** (Map p30, B4; www.winesofportugal.com; Palácio da Bolsa, Rua Ferreira Borges; ⏰11am-7pm Tue-Sat) tasting room is the perfect way to brush up on your knowledge of Portuguese wines (including those produced in the nearby Douro). An enocard costing €2 is your ticket to tasting two to four wines from a selection of 12 chosen from different regions of the country. The friendly, clued-up staff will talk you through them.

wine, you can usually buy a whole bottle (or even send a case home). (Rua de São João 46; ⏰4pm-midnight)

Prova
WINE BAR

25 Map p30, C3

Diogo, the passionate owner, is the man to speak to about the finer nuances of Portuguese wine at this chic, stone-walled bar. Stop by here for a two-glass tasting (€5), or sample wines by the glass – including some beefy Douro reds. These marry well with sharing plates of local hams and cheeses. (www.prova.com.pt; Rua Ferreira Borges 86; ⏰5pm-midnight)

Wine Quay Bar
WINE BAR

26 Map p30, D5

Sunset is prime-time viewing on the terrace of this terrific wine bar by the river. As you gaze across to the graceful arc of the Ponte de Dom Luís I and over to the port cellars of Vila Nova de Gaia, you can sample some cracking Portuguese wines and appetisers (cured ham, cheese, olives and the like). (www.winequaybar.com; Cais da Estiva 111; ⏰4-11pm Mon-Sat)

The Wine Box
WINE BAR

27 Map p30, D4

Wine cases turn the bar into quite a feature at this slinky, black-walled bar. The friendly staff will guide you through the 137 (at the last count) wines on the menu, most of which are available by the glass. They go nicely with tapas like *padrón* peppers and clams in herby jus. (Rua dos Mercadores 72; ⏰8.30am-midnight Thu-Tue)

Entertainment

Restaurante O Fado
FADO

28 ⭐ Map p30, A3

Porto has no fado tradition of its own, but you can enjoy the Lisbon or Coimbra version of 'Portugal blues' into the wee hours at Restaurante O Fado. (📞222 026 937; www.ofado.com; Largo de São João Novo 16; ⏰8.30pm-2am Mon-Sat)

Teatro Marionetas do Porto
THEATRE

29 ⭐ Map p30, B3

A sure-fire hit with the kids (but not only aimed at children), this puppet theatre specialises in shows that range

Understand

Hammer Time: Porto's Mad Midsummer Party

In the sweet heat of midsummer, Porto pulls out the stops, the bunting and the plastic hammers for one of Europe's wildest street parties – the **Festa de São João** (Festival of St John), celebrated in riotous style on 23 and 24 June. If ever the full force of love is going to hit you when you least expect it, it will be here – one of the festival's unique traditions is to thwack whoever you fancy over the head with a squeaky plastic hammer *(martelo)*, though purists still swear by floppy leeks and smelly garlic plants. When it comes to making your affections blatantly obvious, it sure beats the hell out of Valentine's hearts and flowers. For a more subtle approach, there are *manjericos* (potted basil plants with four-verse poems).

As you might expect, these head-spinning attacks of *amor* cause much flirtatious giggling, squealing and chasing in the maze of narrow medieval lanes that spills spectacularly down to the riverfront. Though the exact origins of the *festa* are lost in the mists of time, the *tripeiros* (Porto residents) will tell you that it is rooted in pagan rituals to celebrate the summer solstice and bountiful harvests. And bountiful certainly sums up the city's streets on 23 June, which teem with hammer-wielding locals of all ages scoffing grilled sardines, drinking *vinho*, dancing like there's no tomorrow, and letting Chinese lanterns drift into the night sky.

Avenida dos Aliados transforms into a giant open-air party, with food stands, DJs and live bands whipping the crowds into a frenzy. From here, the locals sweep down to Cais da Ribeira, where fireworks dramatically illuminate the riverfront and the Ponte de Dom Luís I around midnight. Revellers with enough stamina then gradually drift west to the beaches, where the fun continues with partying on the beach, leaping over bonfires (for luck) and dips in the Atlantic at dawn.

While a trickle of locals head to morning mass the following day, the majority nurse their hangovers and head bumps, getting up in time to catch the regatta of *barcos rabelos*, the wooden, flat-bottomed boats that were traditionally used to transport wine from Douro to the port houses – it's the climax of what is Porto's biggest summer bash in every sense of the word.

from fairy tales such as Cinderella to nonviolent political theatre. (☏222 089 175; www.marionetasdoporto.pt; Rua de Belmonte 57)

Hot Five Jazz & Blues Club

JAZZ

30 ⭐ Map p30, H3

True to its name, this spot hosts live jazz and blues as well as the occasional acoustic, folk or all-out jam session. It's a modern but intimate space, with seating at small round tables, both fronting the stage and on an upper balcony. (☏934 328 583; www.hotfive.pt; Largo Actor Dias 51; ☺10pm-3am Wed-Sun)

Casa da Mariquinhas

FADO

31 ⭐ Map p30, E3

Follow the strains of fado to this traditional, highly atmospheric tavern, with live fado nightly from Wednesday to Saturday. (Rua São Sebastião 25; ☺5pm-1am Wed & Thu, 5pm-2am Fri & Sat)

Hard Club

MUSIC

32 ⭐ Map p30, C3

Inside the converted Mercado Ferreira Borges, this happening music club with an industrial vibe hosts acts of great variety – from hip hop and house to rock and tango. There's also a restaurant on the gallery and a lovely esplanade with great views of the square. (www.hard-club.com; Praça Infante Dom Henrique; ☺Tue-Sun)

Shopping

Porto Signs

SOUVENIRS

33 Map p30, C5

A nice twist on the traditional tourist shop, Porto Signs has unique, locally designed graphic T-shirts, as well as Portuguese wine, tea, photography books, cork products and that everpresent Barcelos rooster. (Rua Alfândega 17; ☺10am-8pm)

Chocolateria Ecuador

CHOCOLATE

34 Map p30, E1

If chocolate is the elixir of the gods, this place is surely heaven on earth. Nip in to find a retro-cool wonderland of beautifully packaged Portuguese chocolate bars, truffles – including a deliciously dark number with port wine – pralines, macaroons and bonbons. They make perfect edible gifts. (www.chocolatariaequador.com; Rua das Flores 298; ☺11am-7.30pm)

Tradições

GIFTS

35 Map p30, E1

For Portuguese souvenirs, Tradições is the real deal. In this sweet, friendly shop, the owner knows the story behind every item – from bags beautifully fashioned from Alentejo cork to Algarvian *flôr de sal* (hand-harvested sea salt), Lousã honey and Lazuli *azulejos*. (Rua das Flores 238; ☺10am-7pm)

Ag Jewels
JEWELLERY

36 🔒 Map p30, C5

Housed in an attractively restored 19th-century building, this is a great place to find filigree silver necklaces, bracelets, rings and earrings, some of which are embedded with marcasite. Many pieces have naturalistic and traditional motifs – the Coração de Viana heart, for instance. (Rua Infante Dom Henrique 91; ⊘10am-7pm Mon-Sat, 2.30-7pm Sun)

Prometeu Artesano
HANDICRAFTS

37 🔒 Map p30, C5

A collective of artisans from across Portugal, this antiquated stone-house riverside shop has a fun collection of *azulejos*, ceramic dishes and jewellery (we love the miniature *azulejo* rings), as well as the Portuguese *galo* (cockerel) in different guises. (Rua Alfândega 11; ⊘10am-8pm)

Lobo Taste
HANDICRAFTS

38 🔒 Map p30, C3

A small but groovy shop set in the Palácio das Artes. It specialises in contemporary handicrafts, including ceramic sculpture, wooden radios and a terrific selection of baskets and sun hats. (Largo de São Domingos 20; ⊘10am-7pm)

Top Tip
Two Wheel Porto

If you fancy seeing Porto from the saddle of a bicycle or pedalling along the banks of the Douro to the beach in Foz, you'll find a number of decent rental options in the Ribeira area. These include **L&L** (📞223 251 722; http://lopesrentabike.wix.com/porto; Largo São Domingos 13, 2nd floor; bike hire per half/full day €8/15; ⊘10am-7pm), where the reliable bikes come with helmets, locks and city maps, and **Porto Rent a Bike** (📞912 562 190, 222 022 375; www.portorentabike.com; Avenida Gustavo Eiffel 280; bikes from €10/15 per half/full day; ⊘10am-2pm & 3-7pm), which also has a selection of electric bikes (handy for the hills downtown), children's bikes, tandems and folding bikes.

If you would rather buzz around the city by Vespa, **Oporto Share** (📞220 999 120; www.oportoshare.pt; Rua da Bainharia 20) offers nippy sightseeing tours by scooter.

Explore

Aliados & Bolhão

With a regal beaux-arts boulevard blazing through its centre, this vibrant neighbourhood hides boutiques, old-school grocery stores, pavement cafes and baroque churches dazzling with *azulejos* (hand-painted tiles) down its backstreets. This is where Porto comes to market shop, eat and play, with the Galerias enticing partygoers to its glam-retro bars, sassy cocktail-sipping lounges and live-music venues after dark.

The Sights in a Day

☀ Rewind to an age of lace-gloved farewells at **São Bento train station** (p48), peering up at magnificent *azulejo* panels mapping out Portuguese history milestones. Stroll monumental beaux-arts boulevard **Avenida dos Aliados** (p48), before swinging over to **Mercado do Bolhão** (p61), which thrums with hungry locals shopping for Atlantic-fresh fish and tangy *chouriço* (sausage). Punctuated with boutiques and sidewalk cafes, **Rua Santa Catarina** (p50) is made for a languid saunter – begin at beautifully tiled **Capela das Almas** (p49) and end at sumptuous **Café Majestic** (p52).

☼ Further west, baroque **Torre dos Clérigos** (p49) pops up – climb its 225-step staircase for cracking city views. After a breather, visit enchanting neo-Gothic **Livraria Lello** (p59), a bookstore with a pinch of Potter magic. Revive over more-ish éclairs at nearby **Leitaria Quinta Do Paço** (p50), then check out twin churches **Igreja do Carmo** (p48) and **Igreja das Carmelitas** (p48).

☾ Book a table for dinner at deliciously mellow **Flor dos Congregados** (p51) or literary-flavoured **Book** (p53). Warm up over drinks at retro-cosy **Café Candelabro** (p54) or old-school **Museu d'Avó** (p54), then test your stamina on a **Galerias bar crawl** (p44).

◯ Local Life
Galerias Bar Crawl (p44)

💜 Best of Porto

Getting There

Ⓜ **Metro** Trindade, Aliados, São Bento.

🚊 **Tram** Tram 18 links Jardim da Cordoaria to the Massarelos district. Line 22 makes a loop of the centre between Carmo and Batalha/Funicular dos Guindais.

🚌 **Bus** A number of bus lines converge at the southern end of Avenida dos Aliados and Cordoaria.

Local Life
Galerias Bar Crawl

Ask a *tripeiro* (Porto resident) where the party is at and chances are they'll direct you towards the Galerias, the nightlife hub around Rua Galeria de Paris and Rua Cândido dos Reis. Swinging from retro to boho, urban-cool to alternative, the bars are as busy as beehives at weekends, with the fun spilling out onto the streets. Bar-crawling is the way to go – simply follow your mood and taste in music.

① **Cork Popping**

Bubbles (☎222 086 780; www.bv-bubbles. com; Rua Conde de Vizela 149; snacks €3-4, mains €13-18; ⊗noon-2am Mon-Thu, noon-4am Fri & Sat) is dark, sexy and fizzing with good vibes. Toast the evening with a glass of sparkling wine (from €2) or a champagne cocktail (€7), before mains like Iberian pork loin with Serra cheese and 28-day dry-aged steak. We love the quirky touches: the Mona Lisa with champagne glass in

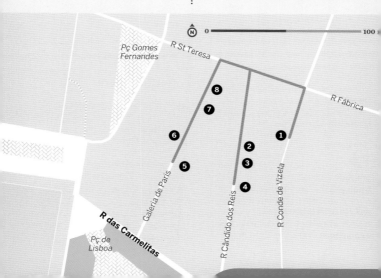

hand (so *that's* why she's smiling) and the champagne cork stools.

2 Urban Cool

With backlit walls featuring a 3D artwork of spirt bottles, high ceilings and a funky world map of names, **The Wall** (Rua de Cândido dos Reis 90; ☺3pm-4am) has a dash of the urban sophisticate about it. Mingle with an effortlessly cool crowd over chilled DJ beats and expertly mixed cocktails.

3 Perfect G&T

The slick, pared-down **Gin House** (Rua Cândido dos Reis 70; ☺6pm-2am Tue-Thu, to 4am Fri & Sat) attracts an upbeat crowd with a splash of class, '80s and '90s pop and rock, and 160 different kinds of gin. Try palate-awakening cocktails – gin and tonic with cucumber and rose petals, for instance, but be aware that some come in fishbowl-sized glasses – more than a couple and the room might start to swim.

4 Culture Club

Plano B (www.planobporto.net; Rua Cândido dos Reis 30; ☺10pm-2am Tue & Wed, 10pm-4am Thu, 10pm-6am Fri & Sat; 🛜) is a creative space with an art gallery in front, a tall-ceilinged cafe out back, and a cosy downstairs where DJs and live bands hold court. Much like the crowd, the programming is truly eclectic, with performance art, theatre and art openings held regularly.

5 Retro Tipples

The original on the strip that's now synonymous with the Porto party scene, the whimsically decorated **Galeria de Paris** (Rua Galeria de Paris 56; ☺8.30am-4pm) has toys, thermoses, old phones and other assorted memorabilia lining the walls. In addition to cocktails and draught beer, you'll find tapas at night. Happy hour (beer or wine for €2) is from 5pm to 7pm.

6 Wine O'Clock

Vintage wallpaper, gilded mirrors and walls of books give a discreet charm to this nicely lit beer and wine bar, **Casa do Livro** (Rua Galeria de Paris 85; ☺9.30pm-4am). On weekends, DJs spin funk, soul, jazz and retro sounds in the back room.

7 Coffee & Cocktails

Housed in a former textile warehouse, narrow, intimate **Café au Lait** (Rua Galeria de Paris 44; ☺10.30pm-4am Mon-Sat) now stitches together a lively but unpretentious artsy crowd. Besides cocktails, there are snacks and salads, including vegetarian grub. DJs and occasional gigs amp up the vibe and add to the good cheer.

8 1920s Paris

A little flicker of bohemian Parisian flair in the heart of Porto, **Era Uma Vez No Paris** (Rua Galeria de Paris 106; ☺11am-2am Mon-Thu, 11am-4am Fri & Sat) rewinds the clocks to the more decadent 1920s. Its ruby-red walls, retro furnishings and frilly lampshades spin a warm, intimate cocoon for coffee by day and drinks by night. DJs keep the mood mellow with indie rock and funk beats.

N

0 ——————————— 200 m
0 ——————————— 0.1 miles

For reviews see
- ◉ Sights — p48
- ✖ Eating — p50
- 🍷 Drinking — p54
- ★ Entertainment — p58
- 🛍 Shopping — p59

R Mârtires da Liberdade

R da Conceição

R de Cedofeita

Tv de Cedofeita

Tv do Carregal

R Dr Ricardo Jorge

R do Almada

City C
Turism

Tourist Police

Praça Genera Humber Delgad

Praça Carlos Alberto

R Sá Noronha

R José Falcão

R da Picaria

R Ramalho Ortigão

Aliados

Av dos Aliado

Av dos Aliados

R Ceuta

Praça Dona Filipa de Lencastre

Avenida dos Aliados

Igreja das Carmelitas

Igreja do Carmo

Praça Gomes Fernandes

R St Teresa

Galeria de Paris

R Cândido dos Reis

R Conde de Vizela

R Fábrica

R do Almada

R Sampa

Praça da Liberdade

Praça Gomes Teixeira

Praça Parada Leitão

Tv do Carmo

R das Carmelitas

Praça de Lisboa

Praça Almei Garre

R dos Clérigos

Igreja Dos Clérigos

Jardim da Cordoaria

Torre dos Clérigos

R Trinidade Coelho

São Bento

Av Dom Henriques

R dos Caldeireiros

R da Vitória

R São Bento da Vitória

R das Flores

R Mouzinho da Silveira

25 22 26 47 38 23 50 52 29 17 27 46 11 24 32 33 10 19 16 20 2 40 41 51 48 34 49 5 6 15 4 3

E   F   G   H

R da Trindade

R do Bolhão

13 ❌

R Sá da Bandeira

R da Firmeza

R de Alves da Veiga

R do Bonjardim

R Fernandes Tomás

7 ◉ Capela
das Almas

31 ⓘ

Ⓜ
Bolhão

R A Braga

R Santa Catarina

R da Alegria

Rodrigues Sampaio

44 🔒
45 🔒

R Formosa

12 ❌

R Sá da Bandeira

43 🔒

8 ◉ Rua Santa
Catarina

R Formosa

39 ✪

Magalhães
Lemos

Praça
Dom João I

30
ⓘ

18 ❌

36
✪

28
ⓘ ▾

14 🔒 **42**

❌
Bruno

R Passos Manuel

21 ❌

35 ✪

Praça dos
Poveiros

R 31 de Janeiro

Igreja de
Santo Ildefonso
◉ **9**

R Santo Il Defonso

R da Madeira

ão Bento
Train Station

Praça da
Batalha

R Entreparedes

R Duque de Loulé

R Loureiro

R do Cimo de Vila

✪
37

R Alexandre
Herculano

Sights

São Bento Train Station
NOTABLE BUILDING

1 ◉ Map p46, D5

One of the world's most beautiful train stations, São Bento evokes a more graceful age of rail travel. Completed in 1903, it seems to have been imported from 19th-century Paris with its mansard roof and imposing stone facade. But the dramatic *azulejo* panels of historic scenes in the front hall are the real attraction. Designed by Jorge Colaço in 1930, some 20,000 tiles depict historic battles (including Henry the Navigator's conquest of Ceuta), as well as the history of transport. (⏰5am-1am)

Local Life
Porto's Contemporary Creatives

Industro-glam emporium **Almada 13** (Map p46, C4; Rua do Almada 13; ⏰10am-8pm Mon-Sat) showcases the one-of-a-kind fashion, decor, art and accessories of five different Porto-based designers and concept stores. Alongside ecofriendly Cork & Co, you'll find funky beach-themed creations from the Yellow Boat, quality teas from Rota do Chá and quirky designs from águas furtadas that are an ode to Portuguese heritage.

Avenida dos Aliados
STREET

2 ◉ Map p46, D3

Lined with bulging, beaux-arts facades and capped by the stately **câmara municipal** (town hall), this *avenida* recalls grand Parisian imitators like Buenos Aires and Budapest. Its central plaza was restored a few years back and often hosts pop-up book, comic and art festivals and exhibitions.

Igreja do Carmo
CHURCH

3 ◉ Map p46, A3

Dating to the late 18th century, this captivating *azulejo*-covered church is one of Porto's best examples of rococo architecture. The tiled panel on the facade pays tribute to Nossa Senhora (Our Lady). (Rua do Carmo; ⏰8am-noon & 1-6pm Mon & Wed, 9am-6pm Tue & Thu, 9am-5.30pm Fri, 9am-4pm Sat, 9am-1.30pm Sun)

Igreja das Carmelitas
CHURCH

4 ◉ Map p46, A3

Blink and you might miss that this is a church in its own right, snuggled as close as it is to the Igreja do Carmo. The twin churches are separated by only a metre-wide house, once the dividing line between the monks of Carmo and the Carmelite nuns. Dating to the 17th century, its modest classical facade belies its lavishly gilded nave. (Rua do Carmo; ⏰7.30am-7pm)

MARK AVELLINO/GETTY IMAGES ©

São Bento Train Station

Torre dos Clérigos TOWER

5 Map p46, B4

Get your bearings and bird's-eye photographs from the vertigo-inducing Torre dos Clérigos. Italian-born baroque master Nicolau Nasoni designed the 76m-high tower in the mid-1700s. To reach the top you must scale its 225-step spiral staircase. (Rua de São Filipe de Nery; adult/child €2/1; ⊙9am-7pm)

Igreja dos Clérigos CHURCH

6 Map p46, B4

Nasoni designed the Igreja dos Clérigos, with its theatrical facade and unusual, oval-shaped nave. (Rua dos Clérigos; ⊙9am-7pm)

Capela das Almas CHURCH

7 Map p46, G2

On Rua Santa Catarina stands the strikingly ornate, *azulejo*-clad Capela das Almas. Magnificent panels here depict scenes from the lives of various saints, including the death of St Francis and the martyrdom of St Catherine. Interestingly, Eduardo Leite painted the tiles in a classic 18th-century style, though they actually date back only to the early 20th century. (Rua Santa Catarina 428; ⊙7.30am-1pm & 3.30-7pm Mon, Tue & Sat, 7.30am-7pm Wed-Fri, 7.30am-1pm & 6-7pm Sun)

Rua Santa Catarina

STREET

8 ⊙ Map p46, G3

Rua Santa Catarina is absurdly stylish and romantic with trim boutiques, striped stone sidewalks and animated crowds. At its southern end it opens out onto the lovely, eclectic **Praça da Batalha**, framed by Nasoni's gracefully baroque Igreja de Santo Ildefonso with its twin bell towers, and the lavishly romantic Teatro Nacional São João (p58), built in the style of Paris' Opéra Garnier.

Igreja de Santo Ildefonso

CHURCH

9 ⊙ Map p46, G4

The gracefully baroque Igreja de Santo Ildefonso sits on the Praça da Batalha. (Praça da Batalha; ⊙3-6pm Mon, 9am-noon & 3-6.30pm Tue-Fri, 9am-noon & 3-8pm Sat, 9am-12.45pm & 6-7.45pm Sun)

Eating

Leitaria Quinta Do Paço

CAFE, PATISSERIE €

10 ✕ Map p46, B3

Since 1920, this cafe-patisserie has given a pinch of Paris to Porto with its delectable sweet and savoury éclairs. Sit in the slick interior or on the plaza terrace for a *cimbalinho* (espresso) and feather-light, cream-filled éclairs in flavours from classic lemon to the more unusual blue cheese, apple and fennel or chocolate and port wine. (⏎222 004 303; www.leitariadaquintado paco.com; Praça Guilherme Gomes Fernandes 47; eclairs €0.80-1.20; ⊙8.45am-8pm)

Understand
The Porto in Potter

If you feel as though you've apparated to Diagon Alley as you duck through the crooked, lantern-lit streets of old Porto at twilight, perhaps glimpsing the theatrical swish of a student's black cloak on the cobbles, you are not alone. There is, in fact, more than a pinch of Porto in Potter.

From 1991 to 1993, JK Rowling lived in Porto, busy scribbling the first draft of *Harry Potter and the Philosopher's Stone* in longhand by day, and working as an English teacher in a language institute in the evening. Word has it that the city soon cast its spell on her, with its moodily lit alleyways, enticing hidden corners and grand cafes – including one of her old haunts, Café Majestic (p52) – which look freshly minted for a Potter film set.

Step into the exuberantly ornate Livraria Lello (p59) and you can't help but think that its twisting staircase might open the door to some hidden passageway or chamber. The neo-Gothic bookshop is pure fantasy stuff. It's crowded with tourists by day, but if you linger here when it quietens in the early evening, you can really unlock the magic.

Cultura dos Sabores VEGETARIAN €

11 Map p46, C3

A hip, healthy addition to central Porto, this vegetarian and vegan restaurant can easily be spotted by the swings in its window. You can help yourself to the lunch and dinner buffet, which often includes hearty soups, salads, wild rice or pasta dishes. Herbal teas and detox juices are available. (222 010 556; Rua Ceuta 80; buffet lunch/dinner €10.50/12.50; 8am-11pm Sun-Wed, 8am-2am Thu-Sat;)

Pedro dos Frangos GRILL HOUSE €

12 Map p46, E2

Frango no espeto (spit-roasted chicken) is the name of the game at this extremely popular and inexpensive grill. Grab a spot at the stand-up counter and join the good ol' boys for a filling meal (abundant chips included). (Rua do Bonjardim 223; mains €3.50-15; noon-11pm)

O Buraco PORTUGUESE €

13 Map p46, F1

As old school as old school gets, this long-standing restaurant on the ground floor of an unassuming office building seems frozen in time, with its polished wood interiors and checkered tablecloths. It draws in a mix of neighbourhood locals and architects for its big and cheap portions of simple fish and meat dishes. (Rua do Bolhão 95; mains €5-10; noon-3pm & 7-11pm)

Flor dos Congregados PORTUGUESE €€

14 Map p46, E4

Tucked away down a narrow alley, this softly lit, family-run restaurant brims with stone-walled, wood-beamed, art-slung nooks. The frequently changing blackboard menu goes with the seasons. Everything from veal to sea bream is cooked and seasoned to a T. The must-try 'Terylene' slow-cooked marinated pork sandwich goes superbly with a glass of sparkling Tinto Bruto red. (Travessa dos Congregados 11; mains €8-16; 6.30-11pm Mon-Wed, noon-3pm & 6.30-11pm Thu-Sat)

Miss'Opo
PORTUGUESE €€

15 ✖ Map p46, C5

Don't miss dinner at this cool guesthouse in the maze of alleyways up from the Ribeira, with a stylishly rough-around-the-edges look and delicious small plates churned out of the tiny kitchen. Reserve ahead, especially on weekends. There are six lovely **apartments** (up to three people €75 to €120, up to six people €145 to €200) upstairs, featuring blond wood and kitchenettes. (☎222 082 179; www.missopo.com; Rua dos Caldeireiros 100; small plates €2-9; ☺7.30pm-midnight Tue-Sun)

Tascó
PORTUGUESE €€

16 ✖ Map p46, C3

Tascó's slick, banquette-lined interior is playfully peppered with personality in the form of a tree-shaped bookcase and a huge blackboard for scrawling messages. Super-friendly staff keep the good vibes and tapas coming – lip-smacking little dishes of *rojões* (pork cooked in garlic, wine and cumin), *morcela* (black sausage), octopus and the like are paired with craft beers, wines and ports. (☎919 803 323, 222 010 763; Rua do Alamada 151A; ☺noon-2.30pm & 7.15pm-1am Tue-Fri, 7.15pm-1am Sat & Sun)

Café Vitória
INTERNATIONAL €€

17 ✖ Map p46, B2

Head to this little-known gem for light bites in the slick cafe downstairs (good-value €6 weekday lunch specials) and heartier Portuguese dishes in the elegant upstairs dining room (open Wednesday to Saturday evenings). There's a pleasant garden out the back, and a festive cocktail-sipping scene on weekends. (Rua José Falcão 156; mains €7.50-15; ☺noon-1am Mon, Wed & Thu, 2pm-2am Fri & Sat, 2pm-1am Sun)

Café Majestic
CAFE €€

18 ✖ Map p46, G3

Porto's best-known tea shop is packed with prancing cherubs, opulently gilded woodwork and leather seats. The gold-braided waiters will serve you an elegant breakfast, afternoon tea or light meals – from a classic *francesinha* sandwich to salads at the healthier end of the spectrum. There's a pavement terrace. (Rua Santa Catarina 112; mains €10-18; ☺9am-midnight)

⦿ Local Life
Portuguese Soul Food

Winging you back to the 1950s, the retro-cool **Casa do Evaristo** (Map p46, G4; ☎222 011 398; Rua de Fernandes Tomás 535; light meals & daily specials €4.50-7; ☺8am-8pm Mon-Sat, 8am-4pm Sun; 🛜) has bags of charisma, decorated with old placards, black-and-white photos and *azulejos* (hand-painted tiles). Take a pew at one of the little wooden tables for lashings of Portuguese soul food – daily specials like *bife à Portuguesa* (bacon topped steak) and *bacalhau* (dried salt-cod) go for as little as €5.

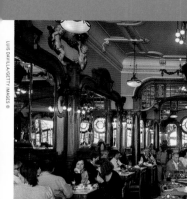

Café Majestic

Book

  PORTUGUESE €€€

19 Map p46, C3

One of Porto's hottest tables, this place has a library theme and buzzes with a mix of well-heeled locals and tourists. The decor is a mix of industrial and classic, and dishes are modern takes on Portuguese mainstays, like baked kid goat with turnip greens, and partridge pie with a ginger and orange sauce. Service can be slow. Book ahead. (☑917 953 387; Rua do Aviz 10; mains €16-23; ☉noon-3pm & 7.30pm-2am)

Café Guarany INTERNATIONAL €€

20 Map p46, D3

With a sunny, tiled interior, marble-top tables and an Afro-Brazilian

mural, this classy affair has attracted the business and literary elite since the 1930s. It regularly has live music (fado and Cuban), and serves decent mains like codfish and fillet steak. (www.cafeguarany.com; Avenida dos Aliados 89; mains €6-15; ☉9am-midnight)

Escondidinho PORTUGUESE €€€

21 Map p46, G4

Amid *azulejos,* dark wood furnishings and starched white place settings, Escondidinho serves solid traditional cuisine to a mainly tourist clientele, hence the slightly inflated prices. Chefs here combine fresh ingredients and a wood-burning oven to create classic dishes such as sole with capers and beef in port wine sauce. (www.escondidinho.com.pt; Rua Passos Manuel 142; mains €15-28; ⏱noon-3pm & 7-11pm)

O Paparico PORTUGUESE €€

It's worth the taxi hop north of town to O Paparico. Portuguese authenticity is the name of the game here, from the romantically rustic interior of stone walls, beams and white linen to the menu that sings of the seasons.

Dishes like veal with wild mushrooms and monkfish are cooked with passion, served with precision and expertly paired with wines. (☑225 400 548; www.opaparico.com; Rua de Costa Cabral 2343; ⏱7.30-11pm)

Drinking

Museu d'Avó BAR

22 Map p46, B2

The name translates as 'Grandmother's Museum' and indeed it's a gorgeous rambling attic of a bar, crammed with cabinets, old clocks, *azulejos* and gramophones and curios hanging from its rafters. Lanterns and candles illuminate young *tripeiros* locked in animated conversation as the house beats spin. If you get the late-night munchies, they also whip up tasty petiscos (tapas; €2 to €8). (Travessa de Cedofeita 54; ⏱8pm-4am Mon-Sat)

Café Candelabro CAFE

23 Map p46, C2

Cool cafe-bar in a former bookstore, with a boho crowd and a retro vibe featuring black-and-white mosaic tile floors, bookcases with old books and magazines, and big windows opening out to the street. It gets busy, with blasting techno on weekend nights. (Rua da Conceição 3; ⏱10am-2am Mon-Fri, 2pm-2am Sat)

Top Tip

Top Snack Spots

Cafe Santiago (Map p46, H4; Rua Passos Manuel 226; mains €5-12; ⏱7.30am-11pm Mon-Sat) Hands down one of the best places to try Porto's classic belly-filling treat, the *francesinha* – a thick, open roast meat, ham and sausage sandwich topped with melted cheese, a fried egg and beer sauce.

Casa Guedes (Map p46, H4; Praça dos Poveiros 130; mains €4-9; ⏱8ammidnight Mon-Sat) Space is tight so be prepared to wait. It's worth it to taste the famous pork sandwiches, served all day.

Padaria Ribeiro (Map p46, B3; Praça Gomes Fernandes 21; snacks €1-5; ⏱7am-8pm Mon-Sat) Snag a terrace table for breakfast, pastries or snacks like *pasteis de Chaves* (puff pastry pies filled with minced veal and parsley).

Understand
On the Tiles in Porto

Azulejos (hand-painted tiles) greet you on almost every corner in Porto. One of the delights of taking a serendipitous wander through the narrow streets of the city is the tiles you will encounter. Old and new, utilitarian and decorative, plain and geometrically patterned, they dance across the facades of houses, the walls of cafes and bars, the tunnels of metro stations and the opulent interiors of churches.

One of the largest and most exquisite panels of *azulejos* covers the Igreja do Carmo (p48). Silvestre Silvestri's 1912 magnum opus illustrates the founding of the Carmelite order.

Stroll along pedestrianised Rua Santa Catarina for a feast of *azulejos* at the Capela das Almas (p49), where a stunning frieze by Eduardo Leite recounts the lives of various saints.

São Bento train station (p48) is a veritable ode to *azulejo* art. Spelling out momentous events in Portuguese history, including the Battle of Valdevez (1140), the arrival of King João I and Philippa of Lancaster in Porto (1387) and the Conquest of Ceuta (1415), the friezes designed by master Jorge Colaço in 1930 are so vivid and detailed you can almost hear the fanfare and the stampeding cavalry.

Praça
BAR

24 | Map p46, C3

The busiest of a string of usually happening bars on this square, Praça is a bit too bright inside, but the marble bar, tropical cocktails (think mojitos, margaritas and caipirinhas) and reggae tunes keep the young and hip lubricated and happy. (Praça Dona Filipa de Lencastre 193; ⏱5pm-2am Mon-Sat)

Casa de Ló
CAFE

25 | Map p46, A2

Hidden off a narrow alley is this boho coffee house beloved by area hipsters. Thick stone walls, old timber-beamed ceilings, a nice little patio out back, funky downbeat tunes and a pretty and pouty artsy crowd. DJs spin on Friday and Saturday. (Travessa de Cedofeita 20A; ⏱2pm-2am Mon-Sat, to 8pm Sun)

Pherrugem
BAR

26 | Map p46, B2

A smoky, dimly-lit den of granite stone, Pherrugem is a stalwart on Porto's alternative nightlife circuit and is jam-packed with locals from all walks of life at the weekend. The music is mostly rock, metal and indie, the drinks cheap and the vibe as chilled as can be. (Rua das Oliveiras 83; ⏱9.30pm-4am)

Aduela
BAR

27 Map p46, B2

Retro and hip but not self-consciously Aduela bathes in the nostalgic orange glow of its glass lights, which illuminate the green walls and mishmash of vintage furnishings. Once a sewing machine warehouse, today it's where friends gather to converse over wine, appetising *petiscos* (€3 to €8) and chilled music. (Rua das Oliveiras 36; ⏲3pm-2am Mon, 1pm-2am Tue-Sat, 2pm-midnight Sun)

Duas de Letra
CAFE

28 Map p46, H4

Artsy cafe overlooking a leafy square, with a low-key vibe, wooden ceilings, an old bike mounted on the ceiling, an exhibition space upstairs with rotating exhibits and two patios. The snacks are delicious, and there's a great tea selection. (www.duasdeletra.pt; Passeio de Sao Lázaro 48; ⏲10am-8pm Mon-Thu, 10am-midnight Fri & Sat, 2-8pm Sun)

Café Lusitano
GAY

29 Map p46, B2

In a handsomely designed throwback to the 1950s, this intimate cafe housed in a former warehouse hosts a good mixed gay/straight crowd. It's a retro-cool space to warm up for a big night out. (www.cafelusitano.com; Rua José Falcão 137; ⏲9.30pm-2am Wed & Thu, 10pm-4am Fri & Sat)

Zoom
GAY

30 Map p46, F3

Located in an old warehouse, this is the gay dance hall of the moment, with some of the best electronic dance music in town and an often-mixed crowd. (Rua Passos Manuel; ⏲11.45pm-6.30am Fri & Sat)

Café Christina
CAFE

31 Map p46, F2

Since 1804, Christina has been bubbling and brewing some of Porto's finest coffee. Take the cue of locals and order a cup of the house blend – it has a kick. A *cimbalinho* (espresso) costs just €0.60. You can also buy beans by the kilo to take home. (Rua de Sá da Bandeira 401; ⏲9am-7pm Mon-Fri, 9am-1pm Sat)

Liquid
JUICE BAR

32 Map p46, C3

For a quick vitamin fix, you can't beat this cool little juice bar, where vitamins are liquidised into detox juices, smoothies and shots. It's also a healthy pit stop for breakfast, wraps, salads and lunch specials (around €6). (Rua do Almada 203; ⏲9am-8pm Mon-Fri, 11am-8pm Sat)

Moustache
CAFE

33 Map p46, B3

Ease into the day gently or wind it out over drinks and mellow beats at this urban cool cafe with cultural

Understand

Street Art in Porto

If only walls could speak... Well, in Porto they do – volumes. Their narrative is that of Porto's growing tribe of street artists, whose bold, eye-catching works emblazon facades. Hurled across crumbling ancient walls, empty storefront glass and neglected stucco, they lend artistic edge, urban grit and an element of the unexpected to the everyday. A far cry from graffiti scrawls, the spray-paint wonders reveal artistic flair and creative expression that transcend convention and stop you dead in your tracks – a stencilled pilgrim and cloaked bodhisattva here, a chiaroscuro portrait and filigree pattern there.

Porto-born or -based artists include the startlingly prolific Hazul Luzah (a pseudonym), who works incognito under the cloak of darkness. His naturalistic, geometric-patterned, curlicue-embellished works dance across dilapidated city walls in the shape of flowers, exotic birds and religious motifs. Other home-grown talent includes Costah, known for his playful, brightly coloured murals; Frederico Draw, master of striking black-and-white graffiti portraits; and the ever-inventive Mr Dheo. Some of the artists are self-taught, others have backgrounds in architecture, digital art, illustration and design.

To click into the scene today, arrange your own self-guided tour of Porto's must-see street art. High on any list should be the central **Travessa de Cedofeita** and **Escadas do Codeçal**, as well as the car park at Trindade, with its large-scale, in-your-face murals. Lapa, just one metro stop north, is another hot spot, as is the gallery-dotted **Rua Miguel Bombarda**. Hazul has left his indelible stamp on **Rua São Pedro de Miragaia**, with a group of 10 artworks inspired by the name Florescer (to bloom or flourish). On **Rua das Flores** clever graffiti sits side by side with beautifully restored historic buildings – look out for vibrantly patterned works by Hazul, glowing neon portraits by Costah and 15 electric boxes – each with its own burst of street art colour. **Avenida dos Aliados** catches your attention with six telephone boxes bearing the imprint of well-known street artists like Costah.

For anyone serious about street art, it's also worth seeing Rua Lionesa, north of the centre in Leça do Balio. It's a giant canvas for the murals of 10 well-known street artists – Frederico Draw and Mr Dheo included – and proof that the passion for this urban art form knows no bounds.

edge. The armchairs are perfect for dawdling over a robust coffee or smoothie and snacks like filled croissants and cakes. Products are mostly organic and fair-trade and they also have lacto-free options. (www.moustache. pt; Praça Carlos Alberto 104; ⏰9.30am-8pm Mon, 9.30am-midnight Tue-Wed, 9.30am-2am Thu-Sat, 2-8pm Sun; 🛜)

Livraria da Baixa   CAFE

34 🖈 Map p46, C4

Part 1920s bookshop, part cafe-bar, this old-school charmer spills out onto the cobbled pavement – a terrific spot for people-watching and eavesdropping over tea or a glass of wine. (Rua das Carmelitas 15; ⏰10am-2am; 🛜)

Entertainment

Maus Hábitos   PERFORMING ARTS

35 ⭐ Map p46, G4

Maus Hábitos or 'Bad Habits' is an arty, nicely chilled haunt hosting a culturally ambitious agenda. Changing exhibitions and imaginative installations adorn the walls, while live bands and DJs work the small stage. Hidden within, there's also an inexpensive vegetarian pizzeria (open for lunch Monday to Friday, dinner Wednesday to Saturday) and a secluded patio. (www.maushabitos.com; 4th fl, Rua Passos Manuel 178; ⏰noon-2am Wed & Thu, noon-4am Fri & Sat)

Coliseu do Porto   CONCERT VENUE

36 ⭐ Map p46, G4

This frayed, yet still stylish, art-deco theatre hosts major gigs – like Simple Minds – as well as grand theatre and dance productions. If something big is going on down here, you'll see posters all over town. (☎223 394 940; www. coliseudoporto.pt; Rua Passos Manuel 137)

Teatro Nacional
São João   THEATRE

37 ⭐ Map p46, F5

The lavish, romantic Teatro Nacional São João was built in the style of Paris' Opéra Garnier. One of Porto's premier performing-arts organisations, it hosts international dance, theatre and music groups. Set in an old synagogue turned church, shows are scheduled sporadically and take place in a spectacular interior courtyard framed by 15m stone walls. (☎223 401 900; www. tnsj.pt; Praça da Batalha)

Armazém do Chá   LIVE MUSIC

38 ⭐ Map p46, B2

This space downtown once housed a roasting company – it's called 'Tea Warehouse' – and now lives on as an alternative cafe-bar with an industrial-chic vibe and a weekly program of live concerts and DJ-spun tunes. (www. armazemdocha.com; Rua José Falcão 180; ⏰9pm-4am Tue-Sat)

Livraria Lello

Teatro Rivoli
THEATRE

39 ⭐ Map p46, E3

In the mood for a musical? This stage serves up mainstream, translated classics, such as *Annie*, from Broadway's yesteryear. (📞223 392 200; Praça Dom Joáo I; 👶)

Shopping

Livraria Lello
BOOKS

40 🔒 Map p46, B4

Even if you're not after books, don't miss this 1906 neo-Gothic confection, with its lavishly carved plaster resembling wood and stained-glass skylight. Feels magical? Its intricately wrought, curiously twisting staircase was supposedly the inspiration for the one in Harry Potter, which JK Rowling partly wrote in Porto while working here as an English teacher from 1991 to 1993. (Rua das Carmelitas 144; 🕙10am-7.30pm Mon-Fri, 10am-7pm Sat)

A Vida Portuguesa
SOUVENIRS

41 🔒 Map p46, B4

This lovely store in an old fabric shop showcases stylishly repackaged vintage Portuguese products – classic toys, old-fashioned soaps and retro journals, plus those emblematic ceramic *andorinhas* (swallows). (www.avidaportuguesa.com; Rua Galeria de Paris 20; 🕙10am-8.30pm Mon-Sat)

Central Conserveira da Invicta

FOOD

42 Map p46, E4

An ode to the humble tinned fish, this store is stacked to the rafters with bold, retro-wrapped cans of tuna, *bacalhau* and sardines plain and spicy. It stocks popular brands like Santa Catarina, Tricana, Cego do Maio, which at between €2 and €4 a pop, make funky gifts. There are always free tastings. (Rua do Bonjardim 136; ⊙10am-7.30pm Sun-Wed, from 9am Thu-Sat)

A Pérola Do Bolhão

FOOD

43 Map p46, F3

Uphill along Rua Formosa is A Pérola do Bolhão, an art-nouveau delicatessen stacked high with sausages and cheeses, olives, and dried fruits and nuts. (Rua Formosa 279; ⊙9.30am-1pm & 3-8pm Mon-Sat)

Casa Ramos

FOOD

44 Map p46, F2

Old-world grocery stores like this one are a dying breed. Besides beans, *bacalhau* (dried salt cod) and *alheira* sausages by the kilo, you'll find everything from traditional sweets to teas and charcuterie here. (Rua Sá da Bandeira 347; ⊙9am-7pm Mon-Fri, 9am-1pm Sat)

Casa Chinesa

FOOD

45 Map p46, F2

This delightfully old-fashioned emporium is crammed with trad-itional Portuguese products: sardines, sausages, dried cod and octopus, *broa de Avintes* (dense corn and rye flatbread), piri-piri chilli peppers by the kilo – you name it. It's also a good spot to stock up on nuts, grains, gluten-free, vegetarian and Asian ingredients. (Rua Sá da Bandeira 343; ⊙9am-1pm & 3-7.30pm Mon-Fri, 9am-1pm Sat)

Goodvibes

DESIGN, FASHION

46 Map p46, B3

Industro-cool Goodvibes is a boutique, gallery, concept store and cafe rolled into one. Stop by to check out the latest exhibitions by Portuguese creatives as well as fashion and accessories – from bold, poppy prints by Hafu to sustainable streetwear by Skunkfunk, backpacks by Eastpack and Ediel cork bags. (Rua José Falcão 107; ⊙1pm-midnight Mon, 10am-midnight Tue-Sat, 3-9pm Sun)

Galerias Lumiére

MALL

47 Map p46, B2

Named after the cinema that once stood here, this mini-mall harbours an eclectic array of original stores, food outlets and pop-up shops, including Sou Sweet artisanal ice cream, Italian deli Luso-Italiana and Vira Retro, with gorgeous notebooks inspired by geometric *azulejo* patterns. Livraria Poetria specialises in books on poetry and theatre, Agu Agu kids' toys and CaCo glazed earthenware. (Rua José Falcão 157; ⊙9am-8pm Mon-Wed, 9am-midnight Thu-Sat)

Vista Alegre PORCELAIN

48 Map p46, C4

Vista Alegre has been doing the finest line in Portuguese porcelain since 1824, with ranges from minimalist to emblazoned with naturalistic motifs. (Rua das Carmelitas 40; ⏱10am-8pm)

Arcádia CHOCOLATE

49 Map p46, C4

Reeling in sweet-toothed locals with handcrafted chocolate since 1933, this gloriously old-fashioned shop is a wonderland of confectionery, with gift-boxed pralines and flavoured bonbons, cocoa-rich bars, and chocolates in the delicate form of hearts and flowers, and almond liqueur dragées – all made with care to traditional recipes. (www.arcadia.pt; Rua do Almada 63; ⏱9.30am-7pm Mon-Fri, 9am-1pm Sat)

Louie Louie MUSIC

50 Map p46, C2

Click into the groove of retro Porto at Louie Louie, well stocked with vinyl and secondhand CDs to whisk you through the entire musical spectrum – from reggae and rock to hip hop, soul, funk, disco, jazz, punk and Portuguese fado. It's cheap and cheerful. (www.louielouie.biz; Rua do Almada 307; ⏱10.30am-7pm)

La Petite Coquette VINTAGE

51 Map p46, B4

Sitting on the 1st floor of a handsome building, this gorgeous boudoir of a vintage boutique is a diva's dream.

 Local Life

To Market

A visit to **Mercado do Bolhão** (Rua Formosa; ⏱7am-5pm Mon-Fri, to 1pm Sat) is a ticket straight to Porto's soul. Almost every *tripeiro* has a soft spot for this 19th-century wrought-iron market hall. At its lively best Friday and Saturday mornings, the market is Porto's larder, doing a brisk trade in fresh produce, cheeses, olives, smoked meats, sausages using every part of the pig except the oink, breads, *tremoços* (lupin beans), *bacalhau* (dried salt-cod) and more. To people-watch over a glass of wine and a sharing plate between purchases, stop by **Bolhão Wine House**, run with a passion by Patrícia and Hugo in their grandmother's old florist shop.

It's stuffed with secondhand designer labels – from Louis Vuitton handbags to Jimmy Choo kitten heels and Christian Lacroix dresses. You might well find a bargain. (Rua Cândido dos Reis 25; ⏱11am-7pm Mon-Sat)

Matéria Prima MUSIC

52 Map p46, C2

When *tripeiros* want to plug into the current music scene swimming away from the mainstream, this is where they go. The record store has plenty of alternative vinyl and CDS too. (www.materiaprima.pt; Rua da Picaria 84; ⏱2-8pm Mon-Sat)

Explore

Miragaia

Sloping steeply down to the riverside, its brightly painted, laundry-strung houses pasted picturesquely to the hillside, Miragaia is a delight for the aimless ambler. Besides a handful of sights and an art-crammed gallery, the real appeal is strolling labyrinthine lanes to sky-high viewpoints, time-warp bars and family-run taverns in the old Jewish quarter, Vitória. Here history seeps around every cobbled corner.

The Sights in a Day

 Make a beeline first thing for the **Museu Nacional Soares dos Reis** (p64) to take a spin around its prized collection of fine and decorative arts, ensconced in the sublime Palácio das Carrancas. The star attraction is *O Desterrado* (The Exiled) by sculptor António Teixeira Lopes. Revive gallery-weary eyes over coffee and homemade cake or a light lunch at bijou **Atelier** (p74).

Now turn your focus to the free **Centro Português de Fotografia** (p66), atmospherically lodged in a former jail. Shutterbugs are in their element gawping at the nostalgic collection of century-old cameras and poignant photography exhibitions. From here, you can easily slip into the warren of narrow alleys weaving through the former **Jewish quarter** (p68).

 Marvel at the cityscape illuminated as seen from **Miradouro da Vitória** (p69), then slip across to **Camafeu** (p76) for outstanding food served with panache in a gracious, chandelier-lit salon. After dinner, choose between an evening spent hanging out with Porto's alternative-artsy crowd at the boho **Pinguim Café** (p77) or gigs and DJs at upbeat **Breyner 85** (p77).

 Top Sights

Museu Nacional Soares dos Reis (p64)

Centro Português de Fotografia (p66)

Local Life

Jewish Porto (p68)

 Best of Porto

Eating

Taberna d'Ávo (p76)

Taberna de Santo António (p69)

Nightlife & Entertainment

Breyner 85 (p77)

Pinguim Café (p77)

Outdoors

Miradouro da Vitória (p69)

Jardim da Cordoaria (p72)

Museums

Museu Nacional Soares dos Reis (p64)

Museu dos Transportes (p73)

Getting There

Ⓜ **Metro** Aliados, São Bento.

🚋 **Tram** Tram 1 (Infante–Passeio Alegre) runs along the riverfront, connecting the city centre to Foz do Douro, stopping at Alfândega en route.

Top Sights
Museu Nacional Soares dos Reis

When it comes to fine and decorative arts, Museu Nacional Soares dos Reis is the mother lode, with a stellar collection from Neolithic carvings to Dutch masterpieces, all romantically snuggled in the ornate Palácio das Carrancas. Requisitioned by Napoleonic invaders, the neoclassical palace was abandoned so rapidly that the future Duke of Wellington found an unfinished banquet in the dining hall. The most striking works date from the 19th century, including sculptures by namesake António Soares dos Reis and António Teixeira Lopes.

Map p70, A4

www.museusoaresdosreis.pt

Rua Dom Manuel II 44

adult/child €5/free,
10am-2pm Sun free

⏱10am-6pm Wed-Sun,
2-6pm Tue

Namban screen portraying Portuguese colonisers in Japan

Don't Miss

António Soares dos Reis Gallery

The museum prides itself on its works by lauded 19th-century Portuguese sculptor António Soares dos Reis. Top billing goes to *O Desterrado* (The Exiled), which is considered the apogee of Portuguese sculpture. Sculpted in Carrara marble in Rome in 1872, this man with a wistful gaze was inspired by a poem of exile by Alexandre Herculano.

Sculpture Collection

Soares dos Reis' sculptures share the limelight with other notable works by 19th- and 20th-century Portuguese masters. Among them is the pensive *Childhood of Cain* (1890) by António Teixeira Lopes, Augusto Santo's *Ismael* (1889) and Diogo de Macedo's bronze *Boy's Head* (1927). Much older is the 3rd-century BC Roman sarcophagus, embellished with a frieze alluding to the four seasons.

Painting Collection

This collection takes a chronological romp through 2500 paintings from the 16th to the 20th centuries, homing in on Portuguese, Dutch and Flemish portraiture, landscapes and religious works. Romanticism and Naturalism predominate. Star works to look out for include Francisco Vieira's evocative *Flight of Margaret of Anjou*, Joaquim Vitorino Ribeiro's serene *Christian Martyr* and Henrique Pousão's chiaroscuro *Woman Dressed in Black*.

Decorative Arts

The 2nd floor showcases decorative arts. Besides fine examples of Portuguese 17th-century faience and 18th-century Chinese porcelain, you'll find intricate 19th-century glassware by Vista Alegre, jewellery (from Iron Age to delicate 18th-century Portuguese filigree creations), and 17th-century Namban screens, which vividly portray the arrival of Portuguese colonisers on Japanese shores.

☑ Top Tips

▶ The museum offers free entry before 2pm on Sundays.

▶ Stop by the shop for quality gifts and the library to buff up on your art history.

✗ Take a Break

The museum's tranquil **cafe** (lunch specials €5.50-7.50; ⊙10am-6pm Wed-Sun, noon-6pm Tue) is a fine spot for a lunch special (there's always a vegetarian option). Or come to linger over a coffee and slice of homemade tart. It opens onto a patio in summer.

Or nip around the corner to Atelier (p74) for a light bite to eat – from freshly made quiches to salads.

Top Sights
Centro Português de Fotografia

It's not every day you go to jail for liking photography. Standing sentinel on the edge of Porto's former *judiaria* (Jewish quarter), this imposing yet muscular edifice built in 1767 was both a prison and a court of appeal in former lives. With the Carnation Revolution and the fall of dictatorship in 1974, it ceased to be a jail. Nowadays it is an eerie, highly atmospheric backdrop for rotating photography exhibitions – many of which have a contemporary, thought-provoking slant.

Portuguese Photography Centre

👁 Map p70, D6

www.cpf.pt

Campo dos Mártires da Pátria

admission free

🕐 exhibition hall 10am-12.30pm & 2-6pm Tue-Fri, 3-7pm Sat & Sun

Don't Miss

Architecture & History

You can sense the weight of history as you wander through the centre. The former cells, including one where prominent 19th-century Portuguese writer Camilo Castelo Branco was holed up from 1860 to 1861 (adultery was his crime, for the record), are now given over to exhibitions. But the sepia photos of one-time inmates are a nod to its grimmer past, as are the impenetrable walls and metal grilles.

Photography Exhibitions

The centre hosts a number of photography exhibitions each year – from portraiture to provocative themes, the abstract to the landscape. The recent line-up featured an exhibition focused on the harrowing world of prostitution in Almería, courtesy of Spanish photographer Rubén García.

Camera Collection

A blast from a sepia-tinted past is the permanent collection of old cameras in the top-floor museum, rewinding to the early beginnings of photography. In an age of smartphone snapshots, it's a reminder of how laborious photography once was. Photography fans are in their element taking in Kodak detective cameras, pre-war Brownies, Century, Varsity and Goldy wonders, early 1930s SLRs and more.

Photography Excursion

Inspired? Why not use your newfound inspiration to take some great photos of your own. Duck down the medieval lanes fanning out from Rua de São Bento da Vitória for street-life shots. Or capture the cityscape during the day and at dusk from the nearby Miradouro da Vitória (p69).

☑ Top Tips

▸ Entry is free, so you can come and go as you please.

▸ Factor in time for a wander in the alley-woven old Jewish quarter nearby (p68).

▸ Look out for the far-from-compact 1900 Penrose Process Camera, one of the largest in the world.

▸ Check out the selection of international books and magazines in the library.

✗ Take a Break

Just across the way, the Casa Santo António (p74) dishes up terrific *petiscos* (tapas) and old-school charm.

Fill up on good honest Portuguese home cooking at family-run O Caraças (p75) on nearby Rua das Taipas.

Local Life
Jewish Porto

The tight skein of medieval alley-ways around Rua de São Bento da Vitória was once the beating heart of the Jewish quarter of Olival, which grew up in the 14th century. Jews made up a third of Porto's population back then, but their numbers dwindled to just 1% after the Inquisition. Dip into the neighbourhood's backstreets to find out more about this remarkable chapter in Porto's history.

① Medieval Charm

With cobbles polished smooth by centuries of shoe leather and pretty tiled houses with wrought-iron balconies, the narrow, gently curving street **Rua de São Bento da Vitória** was the beating heart of Jewish Porto in late medieval times. Keep your eyes peeled for telltale sights of Jewish heritage, such as bronze hamsa (protective hand) door knockers.

❷ Monastic Life

Note the sign in front of former monastery **Mosteiro de São Bento da Vitória** apologising for the expulsion of the Jews in 1496 under the Portuguese Inquisition and the iron fist of King Manuel I. The monastery was built on former Jewish ground in the 16th century by Benedictine monks. Now classified a National Monument, it harbours a beautiful granite cloister and stages performances by the Teatro Nacional de São João.

❸ Azulejo Panel

As you amble down the hill, keep a look out on the right-hand side for the **Casa da Rua São Miguel** (Rua São Miguel 4). On the corner, at No 4, you'll see a panel of 19th-century blue, white and yellow-trim *azulejos* (hand-painted tiles) showing scenes from the life of the Virgin and of everyday life in Porto.

❹ Sacred Sculpture

The **Igreja Nossa Senhora da Vitória** (see p72) stands on land that was once owned by the Jewish community.

❺ Heavenly Views

The **Miradouro da Vitória** (see p72) is a highly atmospheric spot at dusk when landmarks re illuminated and the lights on Vila Nova de Gaia's wine lodges flick on one by one.

❻ Communal Fountain

One of Porto's handful of remaining public fountains, which were once a place to tap into fresh spring water and local gossip, the stone-carved, neoclassical-style **Chafariz da Rua das Taipas** (Rua das Taipas) dates to the late 18th century.

❼ Local Lunch

Swing around the corner and more marvellous views of the city unfold as your path dips down to Miragaia from the Jardim das Virtudes. On the corner is family-run tavern **Taberna de Santo António** (☑ 222 055 306; Rua das Virtudes 32; ⏱7am-2am), which prides itself on serving up good honest Portuguese grub with a smile. It dishes up generous helpings of codfish, grilled sardines and *cozido* (meat and vegetable stew) to the lunchtime crowds.

200 m
0.1 miles

N

For reviews see	
Top Sights	p64
Sights	p72
Eating	p74
Drinking	p76
Entertainment	p77
Shopping	p78

R Ceuta

Cândido dos Reis

R St Teresa

Galeria de Paris

R José Falcão

Praça Gomes Fernandes

R das Ca

R Sá Noronha

Tv de Cedofeita

18

Praça Carlos Alberto

Praça Gomes Teixeira

R de Cedofeita

Praça Parada

12

19

25

Tv do Carregal

Tv de

R do Breiner

Tv do Carregal

R Prof Vicente J Carvalho

22

R Miguel Bombarda

R Dr T Almeida

26

10

R Albert A Gouve

R do Rosário

R do Breiner

24

8

Museu Nacional Soares dos Reis

20

R da Boa Nova

R Dom Manuel II

Lisboa

R dos Caldeireiros

R das Flores

R Mouzinho da Silveira

Jardim da Cordoaria
1

R da Vitória

R dos Caldeireiros

16

Largo de São Domingos

R Ferreira Borges

Centro Português de Fotografia
9

São Bento da Vitória

Igreja Nossa Senhora da Vitória
2

23

R de Belmonte

R da Bolsa

R de Castro

R São Miguel

Miradouro da Vitória
3

15

R do Comércio do Porto

R das Taipas

17

R Virtudes

14 13

21

R São João Novo

Igreja do São João Novo
5

npo dos Mártires da Pátria

R Dr Barbosa de Castro

R A Albuquerque

Passeio das Virtudes

R da Restauração

MIRAGAIA

Calçada das Virtudes

Jardim das Virtudes
4

R T. Gonzaga

11

Largo do Viriato

R São Pedro de Miragaia

Igreja de São Pedro de Miragaia
7

R de Miragaia

R da Bandeirinha

R Armazéns

R Nova da Alfândega

R de Monchique

Largo da Alfândega

Museu dos Transportes
6

Rio Douro

A B C D E
5 6 7 8

Sights

Jardim da Cordoaria   PARK

1 Map p70, D5

This pleasantly leafy park is known simply as 'Cordoaria'. Check out the four haunting sculptures by Spanish sculptor Juan Muñoz. The romantic, narrow lanes that run north from the Cordoaria are the domain of Porto's hippest bars.

Igreja Nossa Senhora da Vitória   CHURCH

2 Map p70, D7

In Porto's medieval Vitória quarter, this church stands on land that once belonged to the Jewish community. Completed in 1539, it was given a baroque makeover in the 18th century following a devastating fire, and features impressive woodcarvings

from this period. The Nossa Senhora da Vitória (Blessed Virgin Mary) sculpture in the altar is the handiwork of feted sculptor António Soares dos Reis. (Rua São Bento da Vitória 1; ◷9am-noon & 4-7.30pm Tue-Fri, 9am-noon & 2.30-5pm Sat, 9am-11.30pm Sun)

Miradouro da Vitória   VIEWPOINT

3 Map p70, D7

Porto is reduced to postcard format at this *miradouro* (lookout), strikingly perched high above a mosaic of terracotta rooftops that tumble down to the Rio Douro. It's a highly atmospheric spot at dusk when landmarks like the Ponte de Dom Luís I are illuminated. (Rua São Bento da Vitória)

Jardim das Virtudes   GARDENS

4 Map p70, C7

A much-loved picnic spot of the *tripeiros* (Porto residents), these tucked-away gardens stagger down the hillside in a series of lawn terraces. Find a shady spot under the trees to drink in the far-reaching views across the city, which reach over the rooftops, down to the river and up to the port lodges in Vila Nova de Gaia. (Passeio das Virtudes; ◷9am-7pm)

Igreja do São João Novo   CHURCH

5 Map p70, C8

Set up a narrow maze of stone stairs, this medieval church with magnifi-

Jardim da Cordoaria

cent views was built in 1539 on land that was originally part of Porto's old Jewish quarter. It's a nice place to stop, take a breath and listen to sad fado tunes riding the wind. (☺8-11am & 3-5pm Mon-Fri, 4.30-6.30pm Sat, 8-10am Sun)

Museu dos Transportes   MUSEUM

6 ◉ Map p70, A7

Set in the gorgeous 19th-century riverside customs house, this museum traces the motorcar from its inception to the future. It does the same for radio and telecom. (www.amtc.pt; Rua Nova da Alfândega; automobile exhibition adult/child €3/1.50, communication exhibition €5/2.50, combined ticket €7.50/4; ☺10am-1pm & 2-6pm Tue-Fri, 3-7pm Sat & Sun)

Igreja de São Pedro de Miragaia   CHURCH

7 ◉ Map p70, B7

One of Porto's oldest churches, the medieval Igreja de São Pedro de Miragaia was completely rebuilt in the 17th and 18th centuries, and pays homage to St Peter, patron saint of fishermen. Its exterior is beautifully tiled with blue and white *azulejos*, which segue through into its light interior. The altar is a profusion of intricate gilded wood carvings. (Largo de São Pedro de Miragaia; ☺3.30-7pm Tue-Sat, 10-11.30am Sun)

Eating

Quintal Bioshop
DELI €

8 ✗ Map p70, B2

Tucked at the back of an organic grocery store, this bright, cheery deli opens onto a terrace and serves healthy, wholesome vegetarian food. It does fresh-pressed juices, creative sandwiches (try the goat's cheese, apple, walnut and honey) and salads. Or stop by for an organic tea with a slice of homemade cake between gallery-hopping on Rua Miguel Bombarda. (Rua do Rosário 177; snacks & light bites €2-7; ⏰10.30am-8pm Mon-Sat; 📶✐)

Casa Santo António
TAPAS €

9 ✗ Map p70, D6

Behind the blue door of this traditional hole-in-the-wall, you can fill up on simple but deliciously prepared *petiscos* (tapas), such as *bacalhau com natas* (salt cod with cream), beans with *chouriço* (spicy sausage) and goat's cheese with honey and ham. If you find a spot, that is; it gets really busy in the evenings. (📞938 704 632; Rua São Bento da Vitória 80; petiscos €1-5; ⏰noon-2.30pm & 9pm-midnight Tue-Sat)

Atelier
CAFE €

10 ✗ Map p70, B3

Just around the corner from the Museu Nacional Soares dos Reis, this white-walled, high-ceilinged cafe is in a beautifully converted century-old building. The friendly couple that run the place rustle up great coffee, sandwiches, quiches, salads and cakes (including a mean apple pie with almonds). (Rua Clemente Meneres 20; snacks €2-6, lunch menu €7.50; ⏰8am-7pm Mon-Fri, 9am-3pm Sat)

Understand
The Sausage with a Story

Found on many a restaurant menu in Porto, the beloved *alheira* sausage is cheap, filling comfort food, whether boiled and served with cabbage and potatoes or – as is more commonly the case – fried and dished up with a runny egg and fries. Taking its name from the Portuguese word for garlic (*alho*), which is often an ingredient, it's a smoky, tangy number, well seasoned with paprika and with an almost pâté-like consistency.

The sausage has a fascinating history. It was first created by the Jewish population during the Portuguese Inquisition (1536–1821), when Jews were forced to convert to Christianity. Jews could easily be spotted by the fact that they didn't hang sausages in the *fumeiros* (smokehouses), so they came up with a cunning plan to fool the Inquisition by inventing a delicious non-pork sausage. The *alheira*, originally a mix of chicken, duck, rabbit, venison, quail or veal and bread, was born. While many versions of the *alheira* now contain pork, you'll still find some that don't.

Taberna do Barqueiro

PORTUGUESE €

11 Map p70, C8

Down by the river, the Taberna do Barqueiro is a rustic, homely bolthole, with a tiled mural of Porto on the wall and a terrace on the cobbles. Daily specials like *bacalhau com natas* and Portuguese-style tapas like sardines, cured ham, cheese and pork in red wine are served with a smile. (☎937 691 732; Rua de Miragaia 123-124; mains €8-12; ☺11am-9.30pm)

Sabores do Sebouh

SYRIAN €

12 Map p70, C2

Nothing flash to look at, Sabores do Sebouh rustles up nicely spiced dishes for pocket-money prices. The owner and chef hails from Syria and cooks fresh with a pinch of love. There's plenty to appeal to vegetarians and vegans on the menu – from falafel to herby tabbouleh (bulgur wheat salad) – and the kebabs are succulent. Cash only. (☎933 446 790; Rua Miguel Bombarda 34; mains around €5; ☺8am-9pm Mon-Thu, 8am-2am Fri & Sat; ✐)

As 7 Maravilhas

GASTROPUB €

13 Map p70, C7

A wood-floored gastropub with a pinch of boho flair, a dash of vintage charm and a generous helping of globetrotter, As 7 Maravilhas is a one-off. The friendly German-Portuguese owners keep the good vibes and international beers flowing. These go very

 Top Tip

Tram Session

Hopping aboard one of Porto's vintage trams is a rickety ride back in time and one of the city's simple pleasures. Only three lines remain, but they're very scenic, especially line 1, which trundles along the riverfront from Infante to Passeio Alegre in Foz do Douro, linking the city and the Atlantic, stopping at Alfândega in Miragaia en route. For the price of a one-way ticket (€2.50), you can take in some of the city's sights from the comfort of a wood-panelled carriage. Trams have been rumbling through Porto's streets since 1872 and were largely mule-drawn until 1904.

well with the tapas on offer, which reflect their well-travelled tastes – falafel, onion bhajis, *currywurst* and the like. (☎222 032 116; www.as7maravilhas.com; Rua das Taipas 17C; ☺1pm-midnight Tue-Sun; ☎)

O Caraças

PORTUGUESE €

14 Map p70, C7

Run with heart and soul by a mother and her two daughters, this quaint, stone-walled tavern is a homely gem. Generous helpings of market-fresh Portuguese soul food – from salt-cod to perfectly cooked pork – feature on the well-edited menu. (☎220 174 505; Rua das Taipas 27; mains €7-10)

Pão Que Ladra
SANDWICHES €

15 Map p70, D7

One of Porto's quirkiest cafes, Pão Que Ladra (Bread that Barks) lives up to its name with a menu etched on a blackboard that is an ode to different breeds of dog. Wooden tables draped with doilies are a homely touch to what is otherwise a cool, artsy pit stop for sandwiches, hot dogs and burgers named after pooches. (Rua das Taipas 8; light bites €3-7; ⊘noon-3pm & 7-10.30pm Mon-Thu, to 2am Fri & Sat, 2-8pm Sun; 🛜)

Taberna d'Ávo
PORTUGUESE €€

16 Map p70, E6

A little slice of authentic rusticity, this stone-walled, softly lit tavern fills up fast at weekends. Do as the locals and order *petiscos* (tapas) like *morcela* (black sausage), *punheta de bacalhau* (codfish salad) and *arroz de feijão* (bean rice). (☎222 012 181; Rua da Vitória 48; petiscos & mains €5-15; ⊘noon-11.30pm)

Casa Garrett
TAPAS €€

17 Map p70, C6

On the street where 19th-century Portuguese poet and novelist Almeida Garrett was born, this trendy new gastro bar is inspired by his masterwork: *Viagens na Minha Terra* (Travels in My Homeland). The menu literally reads like poetry, whisking you on a culinary journey through Portugal with innovative *petiscos* from Alentejo octopus salad to *morcela* with salted Azores pineapple. (☎917 360 616, 222 011 809; Rua do Doutor Barbosa de Castro 56; petiscos €4-8; ⊘7-11.30pm Mon, noon-3pm & 7-11.30pm Tue-Sat)

Camafeu
MODERN PORTUGUESE €€

18 Map p70, D3

Overlooking Praça Carlos Alberto, Camafeu is like dining at a friend's stylish 1st-floor apartment. There's room for just a handful of lucky diners in the chandelier-lit salon, with French windows, antique furnishings and polished wood floor. Dishes like scallops with pear purée, crunchy bacon and walnut salad and codfish with pork cheek are prepared with love, served with flair. (☎937 493 557; Praça de Carlos Alberto 83; mains €14-17; ⊘6-11pm Tue Sat)

Drinking

Piolho D'ouro
CAFE

19 Map p70, D4

Old school, still cool, and crazy popular on weekends when college kids pack the communal tables, lean against thick columns, and sip cold, cheap draughts or strong coffee. Take your poison inside or out in the glass box dining room on the plaza. (Praça Parada Leitão 41; ⊘7am-2am Mon-Sat)

Igreja Nossa Senhora da Vitória (p72)

Gato Vadio
BAR

 20 Map p70, A1

Tucked behind a bookshop, this artsy cafe-bar run by a cultural association does film screenings, readings and occasional dinner parties. There's a nice little patio out back, and it serves cakes, cookies, nice teas and has a full bar. (Rua do Rosário 281; ☺5pm-midnight Wed-Sun)

Pinguim Café
CAFE, BAR

21 Map p70, D8

A little bubble of bohemian warmth in the heart of Porto, Pinguim attracts an alternative, artsy crowd. Stone walls and dim light create a cosy, intimate backdrop for plays, film screenings, poetry readings, rotating exhibitions of local art and cocktail sipping. It's full to the rafters at weekends. (www.pinguimcafe.blogspot.co.uk; Rua de Belmonte 65; ☺9pm-4am Mon-Fri, 10pm-4am Sat & Sun)

Entertainment

Breyner 85
LIVE MUSIC

22 Map p70, C1

This creative space in a two-floor townhouse features an eclectic line-up of bands covering rock, jazz and blues, as well as DJ nights, karaoke and pub quizzes. The large grassy terrace is a treat. Concerts start at around 11pm and entry is free apart from the €3 minimum spend. Sunday night's jam sessions are particularly popular. (📞222 013 172; www.breyner85.com; Rua do Breiner 85; ⏰10pm-4am Wed-Sun)

TNSJ Mosteiro de São Bento da Vitória

THEATRE

23 ⭐ Map p70, D6

Few theatre backdrops are more than the Mosteiro de São Bento da Vitória, which harbours an offshoot of the Teatro Nacional de São João. See the website for the full line-up, which traverses the cultural spectrum from plays to ballet and readings. Tickets generally cost between €7.50 and €15. (📞223 401 900; www.tnsj.pt; Rua São Bento da Vitória)

Shopping

CRU

CRAFTS, DESIGN

24 🔒 Map p70, A2

Allowing Portuguese designers to give flight to their fantasy, this unique gallery space crackles with creativity. What's on offer changes frequently, but at any one time you might find understated fashion, ceramics, accessories, art and beautifully hand-crafted jewellery. (www.cru-cowork.com; Rua do Rosário 211; ⏰11am-2pm & 3-7.30pm Mon-Fri, 2.30-7.30pm Sat)

Understand

Porto's Tripeiros

Spend any length of time in Porto and you'll notice that even locals affectionately refer to each other as *tripeiros*, which literally translates as a seller or eater of tripe. But why? Ask a local and they will tell you different stories, some of which have been passed down as fact over generations.

One refers to the great Age of Discovery in the 14th and 15th centuries when Porto, like much of Portugal, ruled the colonial waves of exploration. Lore has it that the navigators took the best cuts of meat for their lengthy voyages and left behind nothing but offal for the locals. Others swear that the name has its roots from the Portuguese Civil War (1828–34) and the Siege of Porto in 1832, when all the good meat went to the soldiers and nothing but tripe was left for the residents. Others still state that the name comes from immigrants hailing from Swabia and the Czech Republic, who spread their love of tripe in Porto.

One thing is certain, tripe still stars on many a restaurant menu in the form of *tripas à moda do Porto*, a hearty tripe, vegetable and white bean stew, seasoned with bay leaves, lemon, garlic and coriander and mopped up with crusty bread – it's Porto comfort food par excellence.

Interior, Igreja de São Pedro de Miragaia (p73)

Garrafeira do Carmo

WINE

25 🔒 Map p70, D4

Friendly, highly knowledgeable and attentive staff guide you through a staggering array of ports (including many fine vintage ones) and high-quality wines from the Douro, Alentejo, Dão and beyond. Prices are reasonable and it's possible to arrange a tasting. (www.garrafeiracarmo.com; Rua do Carmo 17; ⊙9am-7pm Mon-Fri, 9am-1pm Sat)

O Berdinho

MARKET

26 🔒 Map p70, B2

Worth a mosey if you're in this part of town on a Saturday, this farmers market in the central patio of the CCB has a handful of stalls selling fruit and veg, nuts, honey, preserves, fresh bread, flowers and more. (Rua Miguel Bombarda 285; ⊙noon-7pm Sat)

Explore

Vila Nova de Gaia

Vila Nova de Gaia takes you back to the 17th-century beginnings of port-wine production, when British merchants transformed wine into the post-dinner tipple of choice by dabbling with a dash of brandy. Their grand lodges sit imposingly astride the Rio Douro, inviting you for tours of barrel-lined cellars, tastings and dinner at rooftop terraces with twinkling views of the historic centre opposite.

The Sights in a Day

☼ Trot across the Ponte de Dom Luís I for giddy city views, looking out for the odd crazy kid plunging into the Douro below. You'll emerge high on Vila Nova de Gaia's slopes, where the 17th-century **Mosteiro da Serra de Pilar** (p83) invites exploration. The views from the nearby, palm-speckled **Jardim do Morro** (p83) enthrall. From here, hitch a lift on the **Teleférico de Gaia** (p84) down to the riverfront.

☼ Get versed in port wine at slickly modern **Espaço Porto Cruz** (p83), offering exhibitions and tastings, followed by lunch with a view at **De Castro Gaia** (p87). You can easily while away a couple of hours in the historic port lodges. Top billing goes to **Taylor's** (p84) for its impressive, informative cellar tours (note the eye-popping 100,000L vat of late-bottled vintage) and tastings.

☾ As the last sun creeps across Ribeira's facades on the opposite river bank, pull up a chair for an aperitif at **360° Terrace Lounge** (p88), then head to dinner at **Vinum** (p87) or posher, Michelin-starred **The Yeatman** (p88) – both grant superlative views of Gaia as it starts to glitter.

 **Best of Porto**

Eating

De Castro Gaia (p87)

Vinum (p87)

The Yeatman (p88)

Nightlife & Entertainment

Fado in Porto (p90)

360° Terrace Lounge (p88)

Dick's Bar (p90)

Port Wine

Taylor's (p84)

Graham's (p84)

Cálem (p84)

Ramos Pinto (p85)

Croft (p85)

Sandeman (p85)

Tours

Taylor's (p84)

Graham's (p84)

Cálem (p84)

Ramos Pinto (p85)

Churches, Towers & Forts

Mosteiro da Serra de Pilar (p83)

Getting There

Ⓜ **Metro** Jardim do Morro

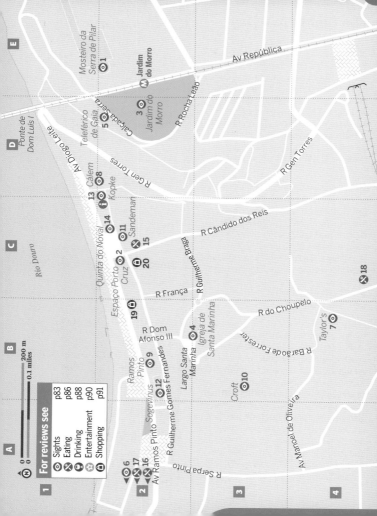

Cloister, Mosteiro da Serra de Pilar

SEAN PAVONE/SHUTTERSTOCK ©

Sights

Mosteiro da Serra de Pilar

MONASTERY

1 ⊙ Map p82, E2

Watching over Gaia is this 17th-century hilltop monastery, with its striking circular cloister, church with gilded altar and stellar river views. Requisitioned by the future Duke of Wellington during the Peninsular War (1807–14), it still belongs to the Portuguese military and can only be visited on the 40-minute guided tours leaving hourly between 10.30am and 12.30pm and 2.30pm and 5.30pm. (adult/child €3/1; ⊘9.30am-6pm Tue-Sun Apr-Oct, 9.30am-5.30pm Tue-Sun Nov-Mar)

Espaço Porto Cruz

NOTABLE BUILDING

2 ⊙ Map p82, C2

This swank port-wine emporium inside a restored 18th-century riverside building celebrates all things port. In addition to a shop where tastings are held (€5 for three ports), there are exhibition halls, a rooftop terrace with panoramic views and the De Castro Gaia restaurant (p87) on the 3rd floor. (www.myportocruz.com; Largo Miguel Bombarda 23; ⊘11am-11pm Tue-Thu, 11am-11.30pm Fri & Sat, 11am-7pm Sun)

Jardim do Morro

GARDENS

3 ⊙ Map p82, D2

The cable car swings up to this hilltop park, which can also be reached by crossing the upper level of the Ponte de Dom Luís I. Shaded by palms, these gardens are all about the view. From here, Porto is reduced to postcard format, with the pastel-hued houses of Ribeira on the opposite side of the Douro and the snaking river below.

Igreja de Santa Marinha

CHURCH

 4 Map p82, B3

In the quaint, alley-woven heart of Vila Nova de Gaia sits this whitewashed church. Built in the 14th century, it was given a baroque makeover in the 18th century by the architect of the age, Nicolau Nasoni. Its high altar displays 18th-century *azulejo* (hand-painted tile) panels depicting biblical scenes.

Teleférico de Gaia

CABLE CAR

5 Map p82, D2

Don't miss a ride on the Teleférico de Gaia, an aerial gondola that provides fine views over the Douro and Porto on its short, five-minute jaunt. It runs between the southern end of the Ponte de Dom Luís I and the riverside. (www. gaiacablecar.com; one way/return €5/8; ☉10am-8pm high season, 10am-6pm low season)

Graham's

WINE TASTING

6 Map p82, A2

One of the original British-founded Gaia wine caves, recently renovated and now boasting a small museum, Graham's is a popular choice for tours,

which last around 30 minutes and are followed by a tasting of three port wines (tour prices vary based on the quality of port you taste). (☎223 776 484; www.grahams-port.com; Rua do Agro 141; tours €5-20; ☉9.30am-6pm Apr-Oct, 9.30am-5.30pm Nov-Mar)

Taylor's

WINE TASTING

 7 Map p82, B4

Up from the river, British-run Taylor's boasts lovely, oh-so-English grounds with tremendous views of Porto. Its one-hour tours include a tasting of three top-of-the-range port wines – your reward for the short huff uphill. Its cellars are simply staggering, piled to the rafters with huge barrels, including the big one containing 100,000L of late-bottled vintage. (☎223 742 800; www.taylor.pt; Rua do Choupelo 250; tours €5; ☉10am-6pm Mon-Fri, to 5pm Sat & Sun)

Cálem

WINE TASTING

8 Map p82, D2

Going strong since 1859, these award-winning wine cellars are among Porto's most attractive. Available in several languages, the informative, entertaining guided tours last around 25 minutes and include a video screening in one of the huge oak vats used for port ageing. A visit concludes with a tasting of two port wines – usually a ruby and a white. (☎223 746 672; www. calem.pt; Avenida Diogo Leite 344; visit to the cellars & tasting adult/concession/under 12yr €5/2.50/free; ☉10am-6.30pm)

Ramos Pinto

WINE TASTING

9 ⊙ Map p82, B2

Right on the riverfront, you can visit the rather grand Ramos Pinto and take a look at its historic offices and ageing cellars. The basic 40-minute tour includes a visit to the museum plus a two-port tasting with chocolates. Tours are offered in several languages. (☎223 707 000; www.ramospinto. pt; Av Ramos Pinto 400; tours & tastings €5; ⊙10am-6pm daily May-Oct, 10am-6pm Mon-Fri Apr, 9am-5pm Mon-Fri Nov-Mar)

Croft

WINE TASTING

10 ⊙ Map p82, B3

This grand hilltop residence houses a rustic cobbled and beamed tasting room that spills out onto a fountain-dotted terrace. Croft has been going strong since 1588. A tasting of three ports will set you back €5, or €9 if you pair them with chocolates. (www. croftport.com; Rua Barão de Forrester 412; ⊙10am-6pm)

Sandeman

WINE TASTING

11 ⊙ Map p82, C2

Housed in an imposing granite building, Sandeman is a perfect first port of call for those who are new to port. It's free to visit the museum, showcasing port-related paintings and memorabilia whisking you back to 1790 when the young Scotsman George Sandeman started dabbling in the port and sherry trade. Guides dressed in black capes and hats lead the tours. (www.sandeman.com; Largo Miguel Bombarda 3; museum free, guided tours incl 2-/5-port tastings €6/16; ⊙10am-12.30pm & 2-6pm)

Sogevinus

WINE TASTING

12 ⊙ Map p82, B2

Sogevinus is the port-wine holding company that owns the Kopke, Cálem, Barros, Gilberts and Burmester labels. This shop stocks a wide array of its ports, around 30 of which can be tasted by the glass. (☎223 746 660; www. sogevinus.com; Av Ramos Pinto 280; tastings per glass €1.30-22.50; ⊙10am-7pm)

 Top Tip

eFun Tours

One of the most fun, ecofriendly ways to zip about town is in a nippy Renault Twizy with **efun GPS tours** (Map p46, B4; ☎220 923 270; www. efungpstours.com; Rua Cândido dos Reis 55). These include the 1½-hour By the River Tour (€38), taking in riverfront attractions from the Ponte da Arrábida to the fishing village of Afurada. The 1½-hour Secret Streets (€38) tour rambles through the historic centre, the 2½-hour Essential Tour (€51) takes in both sides of the river, while the 3½-hour Full Experience (€63) goes all the way to the Atlantic and Foz do Douro. All tours include a cellar visit. The company also arranges walking and cycling tours, and has bike rental (from €6 for two hours).

Kopke
WINE TASTING

13 ⊙ Map p82, D2

Founded in 1638, Kopke is the oldest brand on the hill, but its lodge is not open to the public, which is why you should stop here for the smooth cara-melised bite of a seriously good aged tawny. The 10-year is tasty; the 20-year is spectacular. Port-wine tastings can be matched with Arcádia chocolates or organic olive oil. (📞223 746 660; www.so gevinus.com; Avenida Diogo Leite 312; tastings by the glass from €2; ⊙10am-7pm)

Quinta do Noval
WINE TASTING

14 ⊙ Map p82, C2

Dating back to 1715, Quinta do Noval is one of Porto's most historic cellars,

with its ports and wines hailing from the vineyards on a small estate in the Douro Valley. Tastings by the glass start at €2.50 for a ruby (around €9.50 for a 40-year port). (📞223 770 282; www.quintadonoval.com; Avenida Diogo Leite 256; ⊙10.30am-7.30pm Jun-Sep, to 6pm Oct-May)

Eating

Trezequinze
TAPAS €

15 ✕ Map p82, C2

Wine and port bottles line the walls of this cute hole-in-the-wall bistro, with just a couple of tables and a tiny terrace for sipping a glass or two and nibbling on a sharing plate of Portuguese meats and cheeses. They also rustle up appetising snacks like fish soup, salads and *prego no bolo de caco* – a juicy steak sandwich. (📞964 582 342; Rua Cândido dos Reis 13; petiscos €2-9; ⊙10.30am-8pm)

Dovrvm
PORTUGUESE €

16 ✕ Map p82, A2

Matching a cosy stone-walled interior with a little pavement terrace facing the river, this bistro is literally a stone's throw from the Ponte de Dom Luís I. The friendly staff are clued up about ports and wines, which go nicely with sharing boards of Portu-guese cheeses and hams, and shellfish mains. (📞220 917 910; Avenida Diogo Leite 454; mains €8-12)

Local Life
Ar de Rio

A rectangle of glass and honey-combed steel seemingly teleported in from a future era, **Ar de Rio** (Map p82, D1; 📞223 701 797; www.arderio.pt; Avenida Diogo Leite 5, Cais de Gaia; mains €10-16; ⊙noon-1am Sun-Thu, to 2am Fri & Sat) is one of Porto's most striking examples of avant-garde architec-ture. Mirroring the changing moods of the city and Douro in its facade, it impresses more with its design and views than food – *francesinha* (open roast meat, ham and sausage sand-wich topped with melted cheese, a fried egg and beer sauce) is the menu staple. Or just go for a drink.

Graham's (p84)

Vinum

PORTUGUESE €€

17 🍴 Map p82, A2

Vinum manages the delicate act of combining 19th-century port-lodge charm with contemporary edge. Peer through to the barrel-lined cellar from the pine-beamed restaurant, or out across the Douro and Porto's higgledy-piggledy rooftops from the conservatory and terrace. Market-fresh fish from Matasinhos and dry-aged Trás-os-Montes beef star on the Portuguese menu, complemented by a stellar selection of wines and ports. (📞220 930 417; www.vinumatgrahams.com; Rua do Agro 141, Graham's Port Lodge; mains €16-29; ⏰12.30-4pm & 7.30pm-midnight Mon-Fri, 12.30-4pm & 7.30pm-1am Sat & Sun)

De Castro Gaia

INTERNATIONAL €€

Polished concrete, slatted wood and clean lines give this restaurant in the Espaço Porto Cruz (see 2 ◎ Map p82, C2) a slick, contemporary look. The menu matches ports and wines with *petiscos* (tapas) and mains like octopus rice and pork cheeks cooked in red wine and cumin. There are fine views across the Douro to the houses of old Porto spilling down the hillside. (📞910 553 559; www.myportocruz.com; Espaço Porto Cruz, Largo Miguel Bombarda 23; tapas €3-9.50, mains €9.50-16.50; ⏰12.30-3pm & 7.30-11pm Tue-Thu, 12.30-3pm & 7.30-11.30pm Fri & Sat, 12.30-3pm Sun)

The Yeatman

GASTRONOMIC €€€

18 Map p82, C4

With its polished service, elegant setting and dazzling views over river and city, the Michelin-starred restaurant at the five-star Yeatman Hotel is sheer class. Chef Ricardo Costa puts his imaginative spin on seasonal ingredients from lobster to pheasant – all skillfully cooked, served with flair and expertly matched with wines from the 1000-bottle cellar that is among the country's best. (220 133 100; www.the-yeatman-hotel.com; Yeatman Hotel, Rua do Choupelo; lunch menu €45, 4-/6-course tasting menu €90/110, mains €34-50; 12.30-3pm & 7.30-11pm Mon-Sat, 1-3.30pm & 7.30-11pm Sun)

Drinking

360° Terrace Lounge

WINE BAR

From its perch atop the Espaço Porto Cruz (see 2 Map p82, C2), this decked terrace affords expansive views over both sides of the Douro and the city, fading into a hazy distance where the river meets the sea. As day softens

---

Understand
Port Varieties & Food Pairing

Ruby Aged at least two years in vats; rich, ruby hues and sweet, full-bodied fruity flavours. Goes nicely with cheese and chocolate desserts.

White port Made from white port grapes and aged for two to three years; served chilled. Mixed with tonic water, it makes a refreshing summer aperitif. Pair with salted almonds or crisps.

Tawny Aged for two to seven years in oak casks; mahogany colours, mellow and nutty, with butterscotchy flavours.

Aged tawny Selected from higher-quality grapes, then aged for many years in wooden casks; subtler and silkier than regular tawny. Great as an aperitif or with fruit-based desserts, tangy cheeses and rich pâtés.

Vintage Made from the finest grapes from a single outstanding year (only select years are declared vintage). Aged in vats for two years, then in bottles for at least 10 years (and up to 100 or more). Sophisticated and extremely complex. Enjoy with strong blue cheeses.

Late-bottled vintage (LBV) Made from very select grapes of a single year, aged for around five years in wooden casks, then bottled; similar to vintage but ready for immediate drinking once bottled, and usually lighter bodied.

Understand
Port Wine

With its intense flavours, silky textures and appealing sweetness, port wine is easy to love, especially when matched with its proper accompaniments: cheese, almonds, dried fruit and dark chocolate. Ports are wonderfully varied, and even non-connoisseurs can quickly learn to tell an aged tawny from a late-bottled vintage (LBV). For more insight, take a guided cellar tour followed by a tasting at one of the port lodges.

It was probably the wine-quaffing Romans who planted the first vines in the Douro Valley some 2000 years ago, but tradition credits the discovery of port itself to 17th-century British merchants. With their own country doing feisty battle with the French, they turned to their old ally Portugal to meet their wine-drinking needs. The Douro Valley was a particularly productive area, though its wines were dark and astringent. According to legend, the British threw in some brandy with the grape juice, both to take off the wine's bite, pep it up a bit and preserve it for shipment back to England and – hey presto! – port wine was born. Truth be told, the method may have already been used in the region, though what is certain is that the Brits took to the stuff with a vengeance. They built the grand lodges that speckle the hillside in Vila Nova de Gaia, a testament to their new favourite tipple, and they refined the art of making it – a fact still evidenced by some of port's most illustrious names, including Taylor's, Graham's, Sandeman and Ramos Pinto.

Port-wine grapes are born out of adversity. The vines march up the steep, rocky terraces of the Douro with hardly any water or even much soil, and their roots must reach down as far as 30m, weaving past layers of acidic schist (shale-like stone) to find nourishment. Vines endure extreme heat in summer and freezing temperatures in winter – the ideal conditions to stand up to the infusions. The most common grape varieties are hardy, dark reds such as *touriga, tinto cão* and *tinto barroca*.

Grapes are harvested by hand in autumn and are immediately crushed (often still by foot, the best way to extract aromas and produce wines with balance, structure and depth of flavour). They are allowed to ferment until alcohol levels reach 7%. At this point, one part brandy is added to every four parts wine. Fermentation stops immediately, leaving the unfermented sugars that make port sweet. The quality of grapes, together with the ways the wine is aged and stored, determines the kind of port you get.

into dusk, this is a prime sunset spot for sipping a glass of port or a cocktail while drinking in the incredible vista. (www.myportocruz.com; Espaço Porto Cruz, Largo Miguel Bombarda 23; ⏱12.30pm-12.30am Tue-Thu, 12.30-3pm & 7.30-11.30pm Fri & Sat, 12.30-3pm Sun)

Dick's Bar   WINE BAR

With a private member's club feel, Dick's is a stylish little number at the Yeatman (see 18 ✕ Map p82, C4), with sofas for intimate conversations, live music at weekends and access to one of Portugal's best cellars. Head onto the terrace to sip a glass of vintage tawny or a Douro red as historic Porto starts to twinkle on the oppo-site side of the river. (www.the-yeatman-hotel.com; Yeatman Hotel, Rua do Choupelo 88; ⏱24hr)

Entertainment

Fado in Porto   FADO

Lisbon and Coimbra may be the spiritual home of fado, Portugal's unique brand of melancholic folk music with guitar accompaniment, but you'll find decent performances over a glass of port or two at the Cálem cellars (see 8 ◎ Map p82, D2) every evening. (www.calem.pt; Avenida Diogo Leite 344; €17.50; ⏱6.30pm Tue-Sun)

Understand
Riverfront Festivals in Afurada

Swinging slightly west along the riverfront from Vila Nova de Gaia brings you to the traditional little fishing village of Afurada (p92), reclining near the mouth of the Rio Douro. While the village is in an old-fashioned slumber most days of the year, it springs into action for a couple of spirited festivals in summer.

First up is the **Festa de São Pedro da Afurada** in the days building up to 29 June. Patron saint of fishermen, São Pedro (St Peter) is one of a trio of Santos Populares (Popular Saints) – the others being São João (St John) and Santo António (St Anthony) – who are celebrated with much feasting and merrymaking in midsummer. Dressed in traditional fishing garb, locals parade through the streets with statue-topped palanquins and give blessings to boats along the river. For many, though, it's a great excuse for a monster of a party, with plenty of grilled sardines and *broa de Avintes* (cornbread), *vinho*, live music, dancing and fireworks against the spectacular backdrop of the Douro.

Over a weekend in mid-July, Afurada dusts off its party clothes once again to host the **Marés Vivas** (www.maresvivas.meo.pt), which welcomes big rock and pop names to the stage. Headliners in recent years have included the Prodigy, Lenny Kravitz, Skrillex and fadista Ana Moura.

Sandeman (p85)

Shopping

Casa do Galo
GIFTS

19 🔒 Map p82, B2

An ode to all things Portuguese, this shop is well stocked with gifts from the kitsch to the classy. You'll find the namesake *galo de Barcelos* cockerels, as well as ceramics, textiles (lace and *lenços dos namorado,* or sweetheart handkerchiefs), cork products and edibles like honey, preserves, tinned fish in retro wrappings and, naturally, port wine. (www.acasadogalo.com; Avenida Diogo Leite 50; ⊘10.30am-10pm)

Armazém Lusitano
WINE, GIFTS

20 🔒 Map p82, C2

Besides a decent selection of Douro wines and local ports, you'll find Portuguese goodies like Trás-os-Montes olive oil, Madeira sugar cane molasses, *conservas* (tinned fish) and chocolates – including pralines with port wine – at this stone-walled shop and tasting room. It also does a small line in Portuguese handicrafts. (Rua Guilherme Gomes Fernandes 204; ⊘10am-8pm Mon-Sat, 10am-2pm Sun)

Local Life
Afurada

Getting There

⚓ Local boats make the quick hop across the Douro, departing from Cais do Ouro (near the Ponte da Arrábida) every 15 minutes from 7am to 7.30pm. A one-way ticket costs €1.

Sitting pretty on the banks of the Douro, this breezy fishing village has remained charmingly oblivious to 21st-century trends. Even getting here on the creaking wooden boat crossing the river is like time travel. Afurada is in high spirits in summer when it hosts two must-see festivals – Festa de São Pedro da Afurada and Marés Vivas (see p90).

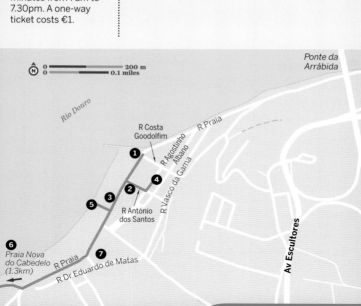

1 River Stroll

The lure of the sea is tangible here, with seabirds wheeling in the sky, washing strung out to dry in the briny breezes and fishers tending to their nets and preparing their tackle. The river is lifeblood for locals. Stroll the waterfront to see a delightfully untouristy side to Porto and enjoy broad views – Foz across the water and the hazy smudge of the Atlantic on the horizon.

2 Market Mornings

Get up early to catch the small but lively fish market, **Mercado de Peixe São Pedro da Afurada** (Mercado de Peixe de São Pedro da Afurada; ☺6am-7pm Mon-Fri, 6am-2pm Sat), in full swing. The fishers sell cod, sardines and other Atlantic catches in rapid-fire Portuguese.

3 Public Laundry

Washing machines are installed in every house, but local *donas* (ladies) still swear by the daily ritual of stone washtubs and good old-fashioned elbow grease at the **lavadouro público** (communal laundry). A blast from a bygone age, this is where they come to wash their whites, natter and sing – a social gathering with abundant soaping and scrubbing. Pop in for a quick nose and to brush up on your Portuguese.

4 Fish Lunch

Fado scales the *azulejo* (hand-painted tile) walls, toddlers tear through the dining room, plump and oily sardines (and other fresh fish) are roasted on sidewalk grills, and you can almost smell the tart *vinho verde* in the air at **Taberna São Pedro** (☎220 993 883; Rua Agostinho Albaño 84; mains €6-10; ☺noon-4pm & 7.30-11pm). There's much to love in this always-packed seafood house, one block inland from the ferry pier.

5 Stylish Marina

Architects Barbosa & Guimaraes have left their imprint on the new **Douro Marina** (www.douromarina.com; Rua da Praia; ☺9am-7pm) complex, a vision in glass and steel with forms that mirror the shape of boat masts and sails. It has a sailing academy, shops (some selling nautical paraphernalia) and cafes, a bike rental place and a day spa.

6 Beach Breezes

Nothing blows away the city cobwebs like a wander along **Praia Nova do Cabedelo** beach, fringed by the protected dunes of the Douro Estuary Nature Reserve. The stiff sea breezes draw kite-surfers here, but it's also a relaxed spot to kick back on the sand and watch the gentle rise and fall of the Atlantic – especially as sunset pinkens the sky.

7 Dinner with a View

Back in Afurada, big river views and warm smiles await at **Forneria São Pedro** (☎227 722 736; Rua Dr Eduardo de Matos 84; ☺12.30-3pm & 8-11pm). Plump for a seat by the picture window in this convivial bistro. The menu is Italian with a Portuguese twist – pizza cooked to thin, crisp perfection in a wood-fired oven and its own take on Porto's beloved *francesinha* (a meat-filled sandwich topped with egg and cheese).

Explore

Massarelos

Low-key Massarelos snuggles alongside Miragaia on the riverfront. If you want to slip off the well-trodden trail, this neighbourhood of breezy views and niche museums will appeal. Slow the pace with a languid stroll in Porto's most fetching botanical gardens, or gallery-hop along Rua Miguel Bombarda, a mile of style with verve, an artsy crowd and global flavours.

The Sights in a Day

☀️ Launch your morning at the port-focused **Museu do Vinho do Porto** (p101), then take a bracing stroll along the river, pausing to admire the *azulejos* (hand-painted tiles) adorning 18th-century **Igreja do Corpo Santo de Massarelos** (p101). Weave uphill for a serendipitous stroll in the **Jardim do Palácio de Cristal** (p96), a gorgeous patchwork of gardens where botanical species thrive, peacocks strut and *miradouros* (viewpoints) command sensational city views. Romance? You'll find it in a nutshell at the **Museu Romântico** (p97).

☀️ Revive over lunch or an aromatic cuppa at hippy-chic, lantern-lit **Rota do Chá** (p99). Now it's time for a wander along the **Rua Miguel Bombarda** (p98), where Porto flexes its creative muscles in cutting-edge galleries, concept stores and artsy boutiques.

🌙 The food in these parts is as creative as the vibe. Mingle with a hipster crowd over nouveau burgers at **BUGO Art Burgers** (p101). Or if you're after more spice, **Frida** (p103) is just the ticket. This art-slung bistro is an intimate spot to wind out the day over feisty chilli-laced dishes and tequila cocktails with a kick.

For a local's day in Massarelos, see p98.

 Top Sights

Jardim do Palácio de Cristal (p96)

 Local Life

Exploring Rua Miguel Bombarda (p98)

 Best of Porto

Eating
Papavinhos (p103)

For Kids
World of Discoveries (p101)

Shopping
Galeria São Mamede (p98)

CC Bombarda (p99)

Museums
Museu do Vinho do Porto (p101)

Museu Romântico (p97)

Getting There

🚋 **Tram** Vintage tram 1 (Infante–Passeio Alegre) stops in Massarelos en route between the historic centre and Foz do Douro.

🚌 **Bus** Useful buses include line 200 (Bolhão–Foz) and 201 (Aliados–Viso), both stopping at the Jardim do Palácio de Cristal.

Top Sights
Jardim do Palácio de Cristal

Sitting atop a bluff, this gorgeous botanical garden is one of Porto's best-loved escapes, with lawns interwoven with sun-dappled paths, dotted with fountains and sculptures, and bristling with giant magnolias, camellias, cypresses and olive trees. It's actually a mosaic of small gardens that open up little by little as you wander – as do the stunning views.

Laid out in the 19th century by German landscape architect Émille David, today the gardens attract everyone from canoodling couples to families, joggers and keen photographers.

Map p100, D3

Rua Dom Manuel II

admission free

8am-9pm Apr-Sep, 8am-7pm Oct-Mar

Don't Miss

Gardens

A mosaic of gardens, from ornamental parterres to secret hedge gardens where fountains gurgle and peacocks parade. There are pockets of woodland and picnic areas, as well as rose and aromatic herb gardens to explore. The Jardim dos Sentimentos (Garden of Feelings) hides the beautiful *Dor* bronze by sculptor António Teixeira Lopes.

Miradouros

On the park's southern fringes are *miradouros* (viewpoints) that grant front-row views of the city. You'll see the Ponte de Dom Luís I loping across the sparkling Rio Douro, the historic centre, and the port lodges cascading down the hillside in Vila Nova da Gaia.

Museu Romântico

On the south slopes of Jardim do Palácio de Cristal, beneath cathedral oaks and sycamores, is the small but stately home where the exiled king of Sardinia spent his final days in 1843. It has been turned into a modest **museum** (Quinta da Macieirinha; Rua Entre Quintas 220; adult/child €2.20/free, Sat & Sun free; ⏰10am-5.30pm Mon-Sat, 10am-12.30pm & 2-5.30pm Sun) featuring the king's belongings, oil paintings and period furnishings displayed in elegant salons.

Avenida das Tílias

The sunlight streams through the lime trees that proudly line this avenue – use it as a central reference point to get your bearings.

Pavilhão Rosa Mota

This striking domed pavilion was built to replace the original Palácio de Cristal (Crystal Palace) in 1956. It harbours a multimedia library, auditorium and cafe, and hosts sport events, exhibitions, theatre and musical performances.

☑ Top Tips

▶ The gardens are at their loveliest in early spring when everything is in bloom.

▶ Come at sunset to see the sky blush pink above Porto and watch the port lodges on the opposite side of the river light up.

▶ To save a bob, visit the Museu Romântico at the weekend for free entry.

✕ Take a Break

Open when the gardens are, the **kiosk** is a chilled spot for a drink and you might spot the odd passing peacock.

It's a five-minute walk to the gallery-lined Rua Miguel Bombarda and the wonderfully boho Rota do Chá (p99) teahouse.

Local Life
Exploring Rua Miguel Bombarda

Proof of the sea-change that's sweeping through Porto, Rua Miguel Bombarda is abuzz with newfound energy and emerging creativity. A nose around its galleries, vintage and design shops, fashion boutiques and retro-cool cafes humming with hipsters reveals a whole new side to the city. If you want to plug into the artistic groove of 21st-century Porto, this is where it's at.

1 **Gallery-Hop**

Kickstart your morning with a mooch around the cluster of galleries at the western end of Rua Miguel Bombarda. Top billing goes to **Galeria São Mamede** (www.saomamede.com; Rua Miguel Bombarda 624; ⊙2-8pm Tue-Fri, 3-8pm Sat), which has a sibling in Lisbon. The gallery hosts rotating exhibitions, such as the recent one spotlighting the abstract, startlingly colourful works of Portuguese artist Gervásio. You might

want to also take a peek in **Galeria Presença** (www.galeriapresenca.pt; Rua Miguel Bombarda 570; ⏱10am-12.30pm & 3-7.30pm Mon-Fri, 3-7.30pm Sat), which hones in on both home-grown and international modern art, with strong ties to Portugal.

② Footwear Fetish

Making a super-chic leap between Porto and Paris, **Tanya Heath** (Rua Miguel Bombarda 498; ⏱2-8pm Mon-Sat) boutique does seriously sexy shoes. The wall is a colour-coded wonder of shoes with – like it! – interchangeable heels.

③ Urban Fashion

A honeypot for hipsters seeking stand-out-from-the-crowd designs, **Cocktail Molotof** (Rua Miguel Bombarda 452; ⏱2-8pm Mon-Sat) raises eyebrows with playful prints, clean cuts and colours that pop. Stop by for everything from urban streetwear to evening dresses and accessories, with brands like Skunkfunk, Melissa, Afracrafts and Ivo Maia.

④ Morning Tea

Interrupt your morning's wanderings with a fragrant brew at heavenly scented **Rota do Chá** (www.rotadocha.pt; Rua Miguel Bombarda 457; tea €2.50; ⏱11am-8pm Mon-Thu, noon-midnight Fri & Sat, 1-8pm Sun), a gorgeous cocoon of a teahouse brimming with boho flair. Join the gallery crowd to huddle around low tables, sample from a 300-plus tea menu and revive over brunch or snacks.

⑤ Vintage Finds

Stop by **Flapper** (Rua Miguel Bombarda 416; ⏱2.30-7.30pm), a vintage and second-hand store, to be time-warped back several decades. Besides clothing and glam accessories – rhinestone-studded clutch bags, kitten heels etc – you'll find ceramics, clocks, dolls and more.

⑥ Design Heaven

Among the galleries along Rua Miguel Bombarda is the unique, independent shopping mall **CC Bombarda** (⏱noon-8pm Mon-Sat). Inside you'll find stores selling locally designed urban wear, gourmet teas, organic cosmetics, jewellery, vinyl, bonsai trees, stylish knick-knacks and other hipster-pleasing delights. The highlight, however, is **águas furtadas** (www.aguasfurtadasdesign.blogspot.co.uk), a treasure-trove of funky Portuguese fashion, design, crafts and accessories. Look out for born-again Barcelos cockerels in candy-bright colours and exquisitely illustrated pieces by Porto-based graphic designer Benedita Feijó. There's a cafe serving light bites in an inner courtyard.

⑦ Art of Illustration

Round out your gallery-hop by immersing yourself in the art of illustration (mostly Portuguese, with some international artists) at **Ó! Galeria** (www.ogaleria.com; Rua Miguel Bombarda 61; ⏱noon-8pm Mon-Sat). Prints range from geometric patterns to wackier pieces – some influenced by Portuguese culture. It does a nice selection of T-shirts, books and postcards.

R Alberto
A Gouveia

R do Rosário

R do Brèiner

R Miguel
Bombarda

R Adolfo Casais Monteiro

11

R da Boa Nova

5

R Dom Manuel II

R da Restauração

Largo da
Alfândega

R da Bandeirinha

World of
Discoveries

R de Mirabala 2

R Armazéns

R de Miragaia

R Nova da Alfar

13

12

Jardim do
Palácio de
Cristal

1

R de Monchique

Museu do

Vinho do Porto

8

Praça da
Galiza

R da Piedade

R de Vilar

R Entre Quintas

MASSARELOS

R da Restauração

10

14

R de Monchique

R Campo Alegre

R Dom Pedro V

R dos Moinhos

R Fonte de
Massarelos

15

7

Museu do
Carro Eléctrico

3

Alameda
Basílio Teles

R do Bicalho

R de Ouro

Rio Douro

2

4

6

16

9

500 m

For reviews see	
◆ Top Sights	p96
◉ Sights	p101
✗ Eating	p101
🛍 Shopping	p103

Sights

Museu do Vinho do Porto

MUSEUM

1 ⊙ Map p100, D4

Down by the river in a remodelled warehouse, this modest museum traces the history of wine- and port-making with an informative short film, models and exhibits. (Port Wine Museum; Rua de Monchique 45; adult/child €2.20/free, weekends free; ⊙10am-5.30pm Tue-Sat, 10am-12.30pm & 2-5.30pm Sun)

World of Discoveries

AMUSEMENT PARK

2 ⊙ Map p100, E4

A sure-fire kid-pleaser, this interactive museum catapults you back to the 14th to 16th centuries when the Portuguese ruled the colonial waves. The latest technological wizardry and a swash-buckling, theme-park-like boat ride re-create scenes of the intrepid seafarers of yore. (www.worldofdiscoveries.com; Rua de Miragaia 106; adult/child €14/8; ⊙10am-6pm Mon-Fri, 10am-7pm Sat & Sun; ♿)

Museu do Carro Eléctrico MUSEUM

3 ⊙ Map p100, B3

Housed in an antiquated switching-house, this museum is a tram-spotter's delight. It displays dozens of beautifully restored old trams – from early 1870s models once pulled by mules to streamlined, bee-yellow 1930s numbers. (Tram Museum; www.museudocarro electrico.pt; Alameda Basílio Teles 51)

Ponte da Arrábida

BRIDGE

4 ⊙ Map p100, A2

Arcing 270m in a single swoop over the Rio Douro and linking Porto to Vila Nova de Gaia, this mighty bridge was designed by prominent Portuguese civil engineer Edgar Cardoso. It was the world's longest concrete bridge at the time of its completion in 1963.

Eating

BUGO Art Burgers

BURGERS €

5 ✗ Map p100, D2

This bright, happening bistro promises to elevate burgers to an art form. It delivers with brilliantly fresh burgers from Black Angus and salmon to veggie lentil and Asian-style numbers – using mostly organic and free-range

---

Q Local Life

Hallowed Explorer

Rising above the riverfront with a facade adorned in blue and white *azulejos* (hand-painted tiles), the **Igreja do Corpo Santo de Massarelos** (Map p100, B3; Church of the Holy Body of Massarelos; Largo do Adro) was built in 1776 on the site of a chapel that was founded by the Confraria das Almas do Corpo Santo de Massarelos in 1394. Prince Henry the Navigator once belonged to this brotherhood of mariners – look out for the great explorer on the tiled panel.

produce. The staff are chirpy, the mood is upbeat and the chocolate cake with berry confit divine. (☎226 062 179; www.bugo.com.pt; Rua Miguel Bombarda 598; burgers €7-13.50, lunch menus €8-12; ⏰noon-3pm & 7.30-11pm Mon-Thu, noon-3pm & 7.30pm-midnight Fri, 12.30-4pm & 7.30pm-midnight Sat)

Casa d'Oro PIZZERIA €

6 Map p100, A2

This concrete-and-glass clay-oven pizzeria leaning over the Douro, just upriver from the mouth, does terrific pizzas including *diavola* (spicy salami and oregano), *Vesuvio* (sausage and broccoli) and *fichi e prosciutto* (prosciutto and fig). (☎226 106 012; Rua do Ouro 797; pizzas €8-12; ⏰noon-3pm & 8-11pm Tue-Thu, 12.30pm-midnight Fri-Sun)

Caseirinho PORTUGUESE €

7 Map p100, B3

A real locals' haunt, and a genuine, great-value pick. Dishes are authentically Portuguese: *arroz de marisco* (shellfish rice), freshly cooked fish and *tripas à moda do Porto* (Port-style tripe with white bean stew). You might have to wait but it is worth it. (☎226 066 222; Cais das Pedras 40; lunch €7.50, mains €8-12; ⏰noon-3pm & 7-10pm Mon-Sat)

Taberna Cais das Pedras PORTUGUESE €

8 Map p100, C4

A warm, homely vision of checked tablecloths and wood floors, this tavern has an appetising assortment of *petiscos* (tapas), such as clams, flame-grilled *chouriço* (sausage), *pataniscas* (codfish fritters) and *feijoada* (bean stew) – all for pocket-money prices. It's worth booking a table for Wednesday's fado evening, which begins at 4pm. (☎222 017 198; www.tabernacaisdaspedras.pt; Rua de Monchique 65; tapas €2.50-5)

O Antigo Carteiro PORTUGUESE €€

9 Map p100, A2

Coyly tucked away on a lane back from the river, O Antigo Carteiro is as close as you'll get to eating in a Portuguese family home. Attentive, clued-up staff pair regional wines with well-executed classics – garlicky octopus, pork tenderloin, *bacalhau com broa* (codfish in maize-bread crust) and the like. (☎937 317 523; Rua Senhor da Boa Morte 55; mains €9-16; ⏰noon-midnight Mon-Sat)

Monchique PORTUGUESE €€

10 Map p100, C4

Down by the river, this restaurant morphs into a bar as the night wears on. Stone arches, art-slung walls and candlelight create a cosy vibe for *petiscos*, seafood and traditional Portuguese mains. There's often live music at the weekends, skipping from fado to jazz. (☎926 714 127; Cais das Pedras 5; tapas €2-9.50, mains €7.50-15; ⏰7.30pm-2am)

Frida
MEXICAN €€

11 ⊗ Map p100, D2

Named after the most flamboyant of Mexican painters, this restaurant spices up Porto's gastro scene. Soft lamp light and walls plastered with Mexican newspaper cuttings and bold Frida artworks create an intimate backdrop for punchy flavours from beef tacos to *chile en nogada* (stuffed poblano chillies with walnut sauce) and zingy tequila-based cocktails. (☑226 062 286; www.cocinamestiza.pt; Rua Adolfo Casais Monteiro 135; ⊙8pm-midnight Wed-Fri, 1-3pm & 8pm-midnight Sat & Sun)

Sardinha Alfândega
PORTUGUESE €€

12 ⊗ Map p100, D4

Lodged in a wing of a former convent, this wood-floored restaurant keeps it contemporary with monochrome hues, backlighting and blown-up food prints. Affording cracking views of the Douro, the terrace is a great spot for drinks before dinner. Fresh fish is the star of the menu, from crispy squid to fillet of Atlantic wreckfish and grouper. (☑931 724 508; Rua Sobre o Douro 1A; lunch €7.50, mains €8-14; ⊙noon-11pm Tue-Sun)

Papavinhos
PORTUGUESE €€

13 ⊗ Map p100, D4

This warm, no-frills, family-run tavern dishes up generous portions of home cooking. Try for a window table to see the river twinkle at night as you dig into classics like clams in garlic and *bacalhau com broa* with a glass of crisp house white. (☑222 000 204; Rua de Monchique 23; mains €9-15; ⊙noon-3pm & 7-11pm Tue-Sun)

Gull
JAPANESE, SUSHI €€

14 ⊗ Map p100, C4

This slinky sushi lounge opens onto a decked terrace overlooking the Douro and a softly lit, wood-floored interior, with bold art. The resident chef keeps the super-fresh sushi coming and the mood gets clubbier at night. Service can be patchy. (☑914 300 038; www.gull.pt; Cais das Pedras 15; mixed sushi lunch €13-15; ⊙noon-3pm & 7.30-11pm Sun-Wed, noon-3pm & 7.30pm-2am Thu-Sat)

Shopping

Kubik Gallery
GALLERY

15 🔒 Map p100, B3

Click into the local arts scene by stopping in at this contemporary gallery, which showcases the work of established and up-and-coming Portuguese and international artists in its rotating exhibitions. (www.kubikgallery.com; Rua da Restauração 2; ⊙3-7.30pm Tue-Sat)

Monseo
JEWELLERY

16 🔒 Map p100, A2

If you're looking for unique, Portuguese-designed jewellery, you'll find just that at this strikingly lit boutique. Many of the pieces are embedded with gemstones or emblazoned with Portuguese motifs. (www.monseo.com; Rua do Ouro 120; ⊙10.30am-7.30pm Tue-Sat)

Explore

Boavista

The city's longest avenue blazes through Boavista, where Porto takes a massive leap into the 21st century, with rooftop bars, urbane hotels and landmarks designed by Pritzker Prize–winning duo Álvaro Siza Vieira and Eduardo Souto de Moura.

The Sights in a Day

☀ No building has more pulling power in Porto than the cultural behemoth **Casa da Música** (p106), a futuristic Rem Koolhaas number that reverberates to the Porto National Orchestra. Traffic whizzes around the monument-topped **Jardim da Boavista** (p109) opposite, while the nearby **Mercado Bom Sucesso** (p110) throngs with *tripeiros* (Porto residents) in search of fresh produce and gourmet snacks. But save yourself for a creative veggie lunch in the hidden garden at **Em Carne Viva** (p110).

☀ Follow Avenida da Boavista west for a walk in the vast, lake-dotted **Parque da Cidade** (p117).

☾ Watch transfixed from beach bar **Praia da Luz** (p118) as the setting sun paints the sky pink. Foz has a slew of fine-dining restaurants, not least the Álvaro Siza Vieira–designed **Boa Nova Tea House** (p118), perched on a clifftop, with Rui Paula at the stove. Finish on a high over cocktails and DJ-spun tunes at **Zenith Lounge Bar** (p113).

👁 **Top Sights**

Casa da Música (p106)

💜 **Best of Porto**

Eating
Em Carne Viva (p110)

Nightlife & Entertainment
Zenith Lounge Bar (p113)

Getting There

🚍 **Bus** Handy buses include line 200 (Bolhão–Foz), 201 (Aliados–Viso) running through Boavista, riverfront line 500 (Praça Liberdade–Matosinhos), and line 502 (Bolhão–Matosinhos), which runs the entire length of Avenida da Boavista.

Top Sights
Casa da Música

All at once minimalist, iconic and daringly imaginative, the Casa da Música is the beating heart of Porto's cultural scene and the home of the Porto National Orchestra. Dutch architect Rem Koolhaas rocked the musical world with this crystalline creation – the jewel in the city's European Capital of Culture 2001 crown. The behemoth conceals a shoebox-style concert hall lauded for some of the world's best acoustics. If your curiosity has been piqued, join one of the daily guided tours.

👁 Map p108, C2

📞 220 120 220

www.casadamusica.com

Avenida da Boavista 604-610

Don't Miss

Striking Architecture

The Casa da Música is a scene-stealer. Harmonious and grand from a distance, its perspectives distort as you approach its facade. Shaped like an irregular polygon, this rough diamond of a building looks as though it has been teleported from another time and place. Carpeted in pinkish-gold travertine marble, the plaza buzzes with skateboarders swooping across its undulations.

Acoustic Marvel

An architectural sensation, the 1300-seat main auditorium, Sala Suggia, uses Nordic plywood, double-curved glass walls and chairs specially adapted to improve acoustics. The hall's name pays tribute to the famous Porto cellist, Guilhermina Suggia (1885–1950). Gold leaf runs through the walls like grain through wood, and it's the only concert hall in the world lit exclusively with natural light – day-time concerts here are special.

Tile Traditions

Rem Koolhaas interplays the links between Portugal and Holland in the striking *azulejo*-clad VIP Room. Adorning one wall are blue-and-white *azulejo* panels replicating those at São Bento train station (p48), depicting the 1415 conquest of Ceuta and national greats like Henry the Navigator. In a nod to his homeland, the other wall is embellished with Delft-style motifs.

Renaissance Room

It's all an optical illusion in this quirky room, patterned with geometric 3D tiles that deliberately throw you off centre. These cubic tiles reflect Renaissance styles, which played on perspective – these again rose to popularity in the works of the Op Art movement in the 1960s.

☑ **Top Tips**

▶ There's only one ticket price per concert as fantastic acoustics mean there is not a bad seat in the house.

▶ Tickets for Sunday morning or midday concerts go for as little as €5.

▶ Be sure to visit the terrace – on clear days you can see the distant fizz of the Atlantic.

▶ English-speaking guided tours at 4pm daily cost €5, last around an hour and give you a great insight into the building.

✕ **Take a Break**

Step up to Restaurant Casa da Música (p111) for swoon-worthy city views and Mediterranean food with a twist.

Take a quick stroll along Avenida da Boavista to petite and pretty cafe Em Carne Viva (p110), with creative vegetarian food and a serene garden.

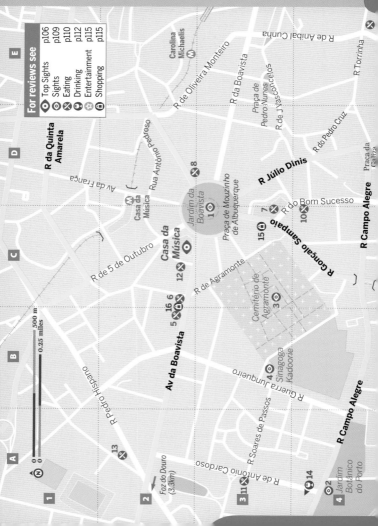

500 m
0.25 miles

R da Quinta Amarela

R de Aníbal Cunha

R Torrinha

Carolina Michaelis Ⓜ

R de Oliveira Monteiro

R da Boavista

Praça de Pedro Nunes

R de J Vasconcelos

R do Pedro Cruz

Praça da Galiza

Av da França

Rua António Pedroso

Ⓜ Casa da Música

R de 5 de Outubro

Casa da Música ◎

⊗⊕ 12

R de Agramonte

16 6
⊗◎⊗
5

Av da Boavista

R Pedro Hispano

Jardim da Boavista ◎ 1

Praça de Mouzinho de Albuquerque

⊗ 8

R Júlio Dinis

R do Bom Sucesso

⊗ 7

◎ 15

R Gonçalo Sampaio

10 ⊗

R Campo Alegre

Cemitério de Agramonte ◎ 3

R Guerra Junqueiro

Sinagoga Kadoorie ◎ 4

R Soares de Passos

R de António Cardoso

⊗ 13

Foz do Douro (3.3km)

R Campo Alegre

3 11 ⊗

⊗ 14

◎ 2

Jardim Botânico do Porto

FXEG JAVIER ESPUNY/SHUTTERSTOCK ©

Monumento aos Heróis da Guerra Peninsular, Jardim da Boavista

Sights

Jardim da Boavista   GARDENS

1 ◎ Map p108, C3

A park at the centre of one of Porto's busiest roundabouts, the Jardim da Boavista provides shade and respite from the hustle and bustle of the city. Its centrepiece is the Monumento aos Heróis da Guerra Peninsular (Monument to the Heroes of the Peninsular War) that commemorates the Portuguese and British victory over Napoleon's troops in the Peninsular War (1808–14). (Praça de Mouzinho de Albuquerque)

Jardim Botânico do Porto   GARDENS

2 ◎ Map p108, A4

Run by the Faculty of Sciences of Porto University, these botanical gardens are a cool escape on hot summer days. Dotted with lakes and flourishing with succulents, roses and camellias, these secluded gardens are the brainchild of port-wine merchant João Henrique Andresen, who had them laid out in romantic style in 1895. (www.jardimbotanico.up.pt; Rua do Campo Alegre 1191; admission free; ⊙9am-6pm Mon-Fri, 10am-6pm Sat & Sun)

Cemitério de Agramonte
CEMETERY

3 Map p108, C3

Opened in 1855 to bury the victims of a cholera epidemic, the Agramonte Cemetery is today one of Porto's most beautiful. The city's wealthiest residents bankrolled its monuments and exuberant mausoleums, some of which are adorned with sculptures by António Soares dos Reis and António Teixeira Lopes. The cemetery is particularly appealing in spring when the camellias and magnolias are in bloom. (Largo de Agramonte)

Sinagoga Kadoorie
SYNAGOGUE

4 Map p108, B3

Sidling up to the Cemitério de Agramonte, the Kadoorie Synagogue is the largest in the Iberian Peninsula and a visible reminder of the importance of the city's Jewish community. It was inaugurated in 1938. For a peek of the beautifully tiled interior and an insight into the workings of the synagogue, hook onto a guided visit of the museum. (www.comunidade-israelita-porto.org; Rua Guerra Junqueiro 340; admission €5)

Eating

Em Carne Viva
VEGETARIAN €

5 Map p108, B2

You can feel the love ooze out of Em Carne Viva like juice from a ripe peach. An elegant stucco-adorned parlour and a fabulously romantic garden set the scene for creative takes on vegetarian and vegan dishes – from the *francesinha* reinterpreted to chunky bean burgers with fries – all served on beautiful crockery. Save room for the divine desserts. (📞932 352 722; Avenida da Boavista 868; 2-course menu €9.50, incl dessert & coffee €12.40; ⏱10am-3pm & 7-10.30pm Mon-Sat)

Casinha Boutique Café
CAFE €

6 Map p108, C2

All pretty pastel shades and hidden garden alcoves, this cafe lodged in a restored 19th-century townhouse is as cute as a button. The food impresses, too, with wholesome, locally sourced ingredients going into freshly prepared sandwiches, quiches, salads, crêpes and totally divine deserts. There's also a deli for take-away Portuguese olive oils, wines, preserves and more. (📞934 021 001; Avenida da Boavista 854; snacks & light bites €3-12; ⏱9am-midnight Mon-Sat, 11am-8pm Sun; 📶)

Mercado Bom Sucesso
MARKET €

7 Map p108, C3

For a snapshot of local life and a bite to eat, nip into Boavista's revamped Mercado Bom Sucesso. A complete architectural overhaul has brought this late 1940s market hall bang up to date. Now bright, modern and flooded with daylight, the striking curved edifice harbours a fresh produce market, food court, cafes and slick design hotel, the Hotel da Música. (www.mercadobomsucesso.com; Praça do Bom Sucesso; ⊙10am-11pm Sun-Thu, 10am-midnight Fri & Sat)

A Loja das Pastéis de Chaves

SNACKS €

8 Map p108, D2

Baked to the original recipe, the *pastéis de Chaves* here are flaky perfection – light, buttery and ideal for snacking on the hoof. Go for the classic pastry filled with spiced minced veal, or other versions which include *bacalhau*, chicken and tomato, vegetable and chocolate. (www.alojadospasteis dechaves.pt; Rua Nossa Senhora Fátima 495; pastéis de Chaves €1)

Oficina - Café Criativo

CAFE €

9 Map p108, E4

A creative space for recycled and reimagined furniture and contemporary jewellery design, Oficina also has a wonderfully chilled cafe for a lunch break or afternoon coffee with homemade brownies. *Petiscos* (tapas) star on the menu and are served on beautiful crockery. There's a deli shop well stocked with Portuguese goodies in case you fancy taking some home. (☑222 010 009; www.oficinacc.pt; Rua Torrinha 151; ⊙10am-8pm Mon-Thu, 10am-midnight Fri & Sat)

Restaurant Casa da Música

INTERNATIONAL €€

This restaurant on the 7th floor of the Casa da Música (see ◉ Map p108, C2) opens onto a black-and-white tiled terrace granting superlative views of the cityscape. Clever backlit art and lofty ceilings create a slick, urban backdrop for bright, Med-inspired flavours, such as sautéed scallops with macadamia nuts, purple endives and chive sauce, and lamb served two ways with polenta and chestnut mash. (☑220 107 160; www.casadamusica.com; Casa da Música, Avenida da Boavista 604-610; mains €16.50-18, lunch/dinner menu €13/19.50;

Local Life

To Market!

Foodies are in their element in the Mercado Bom Sucesso food court, which is perfect grazing territory with stands selling everything from fresh sushi to *piadina* (Italian flat-bread sandwiches), tapas, ice cream and Portuguese sparkling wine. The **Traveller Café** is a good pit-stop for freshly-pressed juices and smoothies or coffee and pastries. If you're looking for edible gifts to take home, stop by **Sabores e Tradição**, which stocks gourmet products from the Trás-os-Montes, such as cheese, olive oil and honey.

The fresh produce market does a brisk trade in fresh fish and shellfish, meat, fruit and vegetables and flowers from 9am to 8pm Monday to Saturday.

🕐12.30-3pm & 7.30-11pm Mon-Thu, 12.30-3pm & 7.30pm-midnight Fri & Sat; 👪)

Casa Agrícola   INTERNATIONAL €€

10 🍴 Map p108, C4

Abutting a chapel, this beautifully restored 18th-century rural house is a splash of historic charm in an otherwise modern neighbourhood. The 1st-floor restaurant exudes old-world sophistication, with its polished wood floor, bistro seating and chandeliers. It's an intimate choice for Portuguese flavours like monkfish *cataplana* (stew). The more informal cafe-bar downstairs has a happy hour from 4pm to 8pm. (www.casa-agricola.com; Rua do Bom Sucesso 241; mains €12.50-28; 🕐12.30-3pm & 7.30-10pm)

bbGourmet Maiorca   INTERNATIONAL €€

11 🍴 Map p108, A3

The muted colours, floor-to-ceiling windows and bistro seating give bbGourmet Maiorca a contemporary look and feel. Go for a light lunch – salads (fennel, smoked salmon and shallot, for instance) and *francesinhas* (roasted meat and melted cheese sandwiches), *petiscos* (tapas), or satisfying Portuguese mains like crispy suckling pig and shrimp Açorda (garlicky bread stew). (📞226 092 003; www.bbgourmet.net; Rua Antonio Cardoso 301; 8am-11.30pm Sun-Thu, 8am-12.30am Fri & Sat; 🕐light bites €5.50-12, mains €13-18)

Restaurante Terrella   PORTUGUESE €€

12 🍴 Map p108, C2

All clean lines, monochrome hues, banquette seating and formica chairs, this city slicker of a restaurant is tucked behind the Casa da Música. It's a relaxed and upbeat choice for lunch or *petiscos*. The €12.50 Sunday brunch is among the best in town – a feast of eggs, bacon, smoked salmon, pastries, waffles and sweet and savoury dishes. (📞910 659 368; Rua Ofélia Diogo da Costa 105; brunch €12.50; 🕐8am-midnight Mon-Sat, 11am-4pm Sun)

Porto Novo   INTERNATIONAL €€€

13 🍴 Map p108, A2

One for special occasions, this refined, modern restaurant in the Sheraton sets the scene with high-back caramel chairs, pristine white tablecloths and ceramic lights. The vibe is sophisticated, the service attentive and the menu skips from wood-oven roasted kid and fresh Atlantic hake to spot-on pizza. The three-course €20 lunch offers good value. (📞220 404 000; Sheraton Porto Hotel & Spa, Rua Tenente Valadim 146; mains €21-29)

Drinking

Bar Casa da Música   BAR

Situated on the top floor of Porto's most strikingly contemporary building, the Casa da Música (see 🎯 Map

Cemitério de Agramonte (p110)

p108, C2), this bar is a fine place to sip a drink as the city starts to light up – the terrace commands great views. DJs occasionally work the decks at the twice-monthly Saturday clubbing sessions (11pm to 4am). See the website for more details. (⏲12.30-3pm & 7.30-11pm Mon-Thu, 12.30-3pm & 7.30pm-midnight Fri & Sat)

New Yorker Bar
BAR

This upscale, contemporary bar at the Sheraton (see 13 ✕ Map p108, A2) is a sophisticated choice for coffee, cocktails and conversing. Retreat to the garden terrace when the weather is warm. Two glasses of wine will set you back €5 during the daily happy hour from 7pm to 8.30pm. (www.sheratonporto.com; Sheraton Porto Hotel & Spa, Rua Tenente Valadim 146; ⏲10am-1am Sun-Thu, 10am-1.30am Fri & Sat)

Zenith Lounge Bar
LOUNGE

14 Ⓜ Map p108, A4

Whole Porto spreads photogenically at your feet from this uber-hip rooftop lounge, which perches on the 15th floor of the HF Ipanema Park. Centred on a pool, the strikingly lit lounge attracts a good-looking, cocktail-sipping crowd, with regular live music, guest DJs and party nights in summer. (Rua de Serralves 124; ⏲10am-2am Tue-Sat May-Oct)

Understand

Porto's Architectural Heavyweights

Porto has become a city to watch on the global architecture scene. Many of the city's newest landmarks are striking in their simplicity and carefully choreographed to blend in with the natural surrounds. Two architects in particular have been instrumental in changing the face of the city and reinventing it for the 21st century.

One name that quickens the pulse of architecture buffs is Pritzker Prize winner and Portuguese starchitect Álvaro Siza Vieira. Born in Matasinhos in 1933, he has designed dozens of buildings and public spaces all over the city – from the minimalist, angular Museu de Arte Contemporânea (p121) to the clean, crisp aesthetic of the clifftop Boa Nova Tea House (p118) and the Faculty of Architecture at the University of Porto, where he graduated in 1955. He has left his imprint on housing projects and office blocks around Avenida da Boavista, the glazed tiles and granite of São Bento metro station, and the Piscinas das Mares in Matasinhos, salt-water swimming pools that snuggle into dimples of the rocky seafront. Under-pinning all of his designs is a lightness and fluidity of form that echoes his desire for continuity in architecture, and his belief that nothing exists in isolation. His work does not seek to dominate but integrate with nature.

Another Porto-born hero and fellow Pritzker Prize winner is Eduardo Souto de Moura, who was taken under the wing of Álvaro Siza Vieira as a budding architect before opening his own practice in 1980. Like his mentor, Souto de Moura has poured his talent into public projects – from revamping metro stations (Casa da Música, Trindade, Aliados and Bolhão included) to the Casa das Artes cultural centre where he finds expression in natural materials and purity of form. Among his other standouts are the Burgo Tower (2007), with the dual character of its facade – juxtaposing horizontal with vertical, opaque with transparent. More playful still is his space-age Casa do Cinema Manoel da Oliveira in Foz, a futuristically modernist edifice with protruding windows.

The dream duo finely tuned their act before exporting it overseas, col-laborating on numerous projects together – from London's curvaceous, lattice-work Serpentine Gallery Pavilion in 2005 to the *Sensing Spaces* exhibition at the Royal Academy in 2014. For a self-guided tour of their Porto creations, pick up the free architecture maps and guides at the tourist office. And for more on the city's architecture, see p141.

Entertainment

Casa da Música
LIVE MUSIC

Grand and minimalist, sophisticated yet populist, Porto's music mecca is the Casa da Música (see 👁 Map p108, C2), with a shoebox-style concert hall at its heart, meticulously engineered to accommodate everything from jazz duets to Beethoven's Ninth. The hall holds concerts most nights of the year, from classical and jazz to fado and electronica, with occasional summer concerts staged outdoors in the adjoining plaza. (House of Music; 📞220 120 220; www.casadamusica.com; Avenida da Boavista 604)

Shopping

Península Boutique Center
MALL

15 🔒 Map p108, C3

This modern mall harbours a range of Portuguese and international brands, with a focus on fashion and labels like Massimo Dutti, Adolfo Dominguez, Elena Mirò and Purificación García, as well as a handful of jewellers, a perfumery and a cafe, Ponto K. (www.peninsula.pt; Praça do Bom Sucesso 159; ⏰10am-10pm Mon-Sat, 10am-8pm Sun; 🛜)

Algo by Colonial
SWEETS

Take home traditional French and Portuguese patisserie and delectable pralines from this confectionery shop by the entrance to Mercado Bom Sucesso (see 7 🍴 Map p108, C3). (Praça Bom Sucesso; ⏰10am-11pm Sun-Thu, 10am-midnight Fri & Sat)

Nuno Balthazar
FASHION

16 🔒 Map p108, C2

This is the flagship of designer Nuno Balthazar, Portugal's king of the catwalk. Pop in to take a look at his latest collections, which are always urbanely elegant and beautifully cut. (📞226 054 982; www.nunobalthazar.com; Avenida da Boavista 856; ⏰10.30am-7.30pm Mon-Sat)

Local Life
Foz do Douro

Out west, Foz do Douro moves to its own relaxed beat, with *en vogue* beach bars humming with bronzed locals, an Atlantic-thrashed esplanade and fine-dining restaurants. Wander the esplanade to the backbeat of the crashing Atlantic and kick back on the beach with an ice cream.

Getting There

🚋 **Tram** Vintage tram 1 (Infante–Passeio Alegre) trundles between the historic centre and Foz do Douro.

❶ Park Life

The hum of traffic on Avenida da Boavista fades as you enter the serene, green **Parque da Cidade** (Avenida da Boavista), Portugal's largest urban park. With 10km of walking and cycling trails, this is where locals come to unplug and recharge, picnic, play ball, jog, cycle, lounge in the sun and feed the ducks in the lake.

❷ The Fort

Otherwise known as the Castelo do Queijo (Cheese Castle) because of the wedge of rock it stands upon, **Forte de São Francisco Xavier** (Praça Gonçalves Zarco; admission €0.50; ⏱1-6pm Tue-Sun) looks every inch the archetypal fortress with its sturdy ramparts, watchtowers and drawbridge. Built in 1661, it harbours a small weaponry exhibition, but more impressive is the view reaching out to sea – sunset is prime time.

❸ Sealife

Some 5000 marine creatures splash in the tanks at **Sealife Porto** (www.visitsealife.com; 1 Rua Particular do Castelo do Queijo; adult/child €13/9; ⏱10am-6pm Mon-Fri, 10am-7pm Sat & Sun; 👶), where highlights include a shark tunnel and a rock pool for handling crabs, starfish and sea urchins. Aquatic oddities include glow-in-the-dark jellyfish, South American leaf fish and cow-nosed rays. The sharks are fed at 11am and 2pm sharp, the rays at noon and 4pm.

❹ The Lighthouse

One of Foz' most visible icons, **Farol Senhora da Luz** (Avenida Dom Carlos I) stands on an esplanade, bearing the full brunt of the swells and storms of the Atlantic. Take a bracing stroll here for big views of ocean and sky.

❺ Garden Ambling

A joy for the aimless ambler, the 19th-century **Jardim do Passeio Alegre** (Rua Passeio Alegre) is flanked by graceful old buildings and dotted with willowy palms, sculptures, fountains and a bandstand that occasionally stages concerts in summer. Listen to the crash of the ocean as you wander its tree-canopied avenues. There's also crazy golf for the kids.

❻ Sea-View Lunch

Alluring views of the thrashing Atlantic draw Porto locals to the terrace of **Tavi** (www.tavi.pt; Rua Senhora da Luz 363; snacks, sweets & light mains €2-12; ⏱7.30am-11pm Mon-Thu, 7.30am-midnight Fri & Sat, 8am-8pm Sun, shorter hours low season), a renowned seafront patisserie that has recently had a bright and breezy makeover. It rustles up light mains, creative salads and savoury crêpes, but is best known for its sweet confections: chocolates, ice cream, traditional Portuguese *bolo de arroz* (rice cakes), patisserie and good strong coffee.

❼ Waterfront Dining

Right on the waterfront is **Casa de Pasto da Palmeira** (📞226 168 244; Rua do Passeio Alegre 450; mains €6.50-14; ⏱noon-midnight Tue-Sun), which has two small colourful rooms featuring contemporary artwork and a few tables on the front patio. The creative small-size dishes change daily – think hake and shrimp *moqueca* (Brazilian fish stew) with banana and coriander, and *alheira* (light, garlicky sausage of poultry or game) rolls with turnip sprouts.

8 Modern Eating

Hidden away from the seafront, **Cafeína** (☎226 108 059; www.cafeina.pt; Rua do Padrão 100; mains €14-19; ⏰12.30-6pm & 7.30pm-12.30am Sun-Thu, to 1.30am Fri & Sat; 🅿) has a touch of class, with soft light, moss-green walls, crisp tablecloths, lustrous wood floors and bookcases. The food is best described as modern European, simple as stuffed squid with saffron purée and rack of lamb in a herb and lemon crust, expertly matched with Portuguese wines.

9 Ichiban

Ichiban (☎226 186 111; www.ichiban.pt; Avenida do Brasil 454; sushi & sashimi sets €12-45; ⏰12.30-3pm & 7-11pm Tue-Thu, 12.30-3pm & 7.30pm-1am Fri & Sat, 12.30-3pm Sun) is a sleek, bright space where the sushi, sashimi and maki is as fresh as it comes.

10 Pedro Lemos

One of Porto's two Michelin-starred restaurants, **Pedro Lemos** (☎220 115 986; www.pedrolemos.net; Rua do Padre Luís Cabral 974; 3- to 7-course menus €55-90; ⏰12.30-3pm & 7.30-11pm Tue-Sun) is sheer delight. With a love of seasonal sourcing and robust flavours, the namesake chef creates culinary fireworks using first-class ingredients, be it ultra-fresh Atlantic bivalves or Alentejano black pork cooked to smoky deliciousness with wild mushrooms. Choose between the subtly lit, cosy-chic dining room or the roof terrace.

11 Coastal Drinks

Praia da Luz (www.praiadaluz.pt; Avenida Brasil; ⏰9am-2am) is a worthwhile stop when out exploring Porto's coastline. It rambles over tiered wooden decks to

---

Understand
Culinary Highs

Designed by prizewinning Portuguese architect Álvaro Siza Vieira and completed in 1963, the cliffside **Boa Nova Tea House** (☎932 499 444, 229 940 066; www.ruipaula.com; Avenida da Liberdade, Leça da Palmeira, Matosinhos; ⏰7-11pm Mon, 12.30-3pm & 7-11pm Tue-Sat), also known as the Casa de Cha, is set above a crashing sea. Massive boulders frame the white, low-rise building, while inside the Zenlike design continues as light floods the polished wood and stone interior.

Porto star chef Rui Paula took to the stove in 2014, and brings lightness of touch, a careful eye for sourcing and a flair for presentation to winningly fresh fish and seafood dishes, giving dishes like locally caught crab and codfish a pinch of wow factor.

The restaurant sits near the lighthouse in Matosinhos, just north of Foz do Douro along the coast. It's best reached by car or taxi.

its own private rocky cove, and while you should probably skip the food, you should definitely enjoy a cocktail. Bring a sweater. It's about 500m north of the Castelo de São João.

12 Clubbing

Basement club **Industria** (Avenida do Brasil 843; ☾midnight-6am Fri & Sat), owned by Antonio Pereira (aka DJ Vibe), his girlfriend and Portugal celebrity, Merche Romer, was recently remodelled and still serves up deep house to a crowd that generally skews young. Take bus 1M and get off at the Molhe stop.

13 Pubbing

Right on the seafront, **Bonaparte** (Avenida do Brasil 130; ☾5pm-2am) is a shipshape pub with a warm, woody, lantern-lit interior. It's a cosy, nicely relaxed spot for a pint of Guinness.

14 Picnic Supplies

Fancy packing up a picnic for the beach? You'll find all you need at **Augusto Leite** (Rua do Passeio Alegre 924; ☾9am-8.30pm Mon-Sat), a delightful family-run deli, grocery store and wine shop. Besides Portuguese and international cheeses, cured meats and sweets, there's excellent wood-fired bread from the Trás-os-Montes.

15 Foz Market

For a bite to eat, stop by **Mercado da Foz** (Rua de Diu; ☾7am-1pm Mon & Sat, 7am-7pm Tue-Fri), where you can sample (and buy) Trás-os-Montes cheeses and smoked sausages, Douro wines and meltingly tender *leitão* (suckling pig).

Understand
Beach Time in Foz

While they can't quite rival Portugal's best, Foz has a trio of decent (if rocky) beaches, great for lounging in the sun, strolling along the esplanade and taking a refreshing paddle. All have been awarded a Blue Flag for cleanliness. This is where locals come to unplug and recharge, so you'll find that they are at their busiest on hot summer weekends. On quiet weekdays in low season you'll have the sands pretty much to yourself. The beaches are also prime spots for watching the sun plop into the wave-lashed Atlantic at sunset over a cocktail by the water's edge.

First up is the generously sized strip of sand, **Praia da Luz**, fringed by an esplanade and backed by cafes and restaurants. It nudges up to **Praia de Gondarém**, a slim strip of sand that disappears at high tide. It sidles up to **Praia da Molhe**, a wider wedge of beach, easily identified by the columns of the 1930s Pérgola da Foz, where the promenade perfectly frames the ocean.

16 Beachside Boutique

A fashion boutique, interior design and concept store rolled into one urban-cool whole, **The Yellow Boat** (www.theyellowboatstore.com; Rua Rui Barbosa 21; ☾3-7pm Mon, 11am-1pm & 3-7pm Tue-Sat) sells – among other things – objects that are inspired by the sea, summer and beach.

Top Sights
Serralves

Getting There

The estate and museum are 6km west of the city centre.

M **Metro** Exit at Casa da Música, where there are onward connections on buses 201, 203, 502 and 504 at the Boavista Rotunda.

This arrestingly minimalist, whitewashed space was designed by the eminent Porto-born architect Álvaro Siza Vieira in 1999 and classified a National Monument in 2012. Despite its out-of-the-way location on Porto's western fringes, it is one of Portugal's most-visited museums and an absolute must-see for fans of contemporary art. Besides the gallery, there is the pristine art-deco villa, Casa de Serralves, to explore and an 18-hectare park dotted with sculptures, a lake and pockets of woodland to roam.

Casa de Serralves

Don't Miss

Cutting-Edge Architecture

Cutting-edge architecturally and artistically, the Museu de Arte Contemporânea is the brainchild of Pritzker Prize–winning architect Álvaro Siza, born in nearby Matasinhos. The U-shaped museum displays his trademark clean lines, playful heights and textures and use of natural materials – granite, oak and marble – all of which creates a seamless interplay between the gallery and gardens.

Museu de Arte Contemporânea

Porto's answer to the Guggenheim, the museum draws on its permanent collection (featuring works from the late 1960s to the present) and ventures further afield to stage first-rate exhibitions of contemporary art. Geometric mirror works by Iranian artist Monir Shahroudy Farmanfarmaian and the post-war works of Brazilian modernist painter Mira Shendel have been in the spotlight recently.

Parque de Serralves

Centred on a lake, this park enlivens museum-weary eyes. It's a delight to wander its ornamental parterres, beech groves, birch glades and avenues lined with sequoias and sweet gum trees. Find shade in pockets of greenery nurturing roses and camellias. The gardens are liberally scattered with sculptures, including the much-photographed giant shovel, *Plantoir*, by Claes Oldenburg.

Casa de Serralves

The powder-puff pink Casa de Serralves is one of Portugal's most striking examples of art-deco style. It was built between 1925 and 1944 for the Count of Vizela, Carlos Alberto Cabral, a man of refined French tastes, who enlisted the top architects and designers of the age – René Lalique designed the skylight.

www.serralves.pt

Rua Dom João de Castro 210

adult/child museums & park €8.50/free, park €4/free

⊙10am-7pm Tue-Fri, 10am-8pm Sat & Sun, shorter hours in winter

☑ Top Tips

▶ Allow at least half a day to do Serralves justice – this isn't a sight to rush.

▶ Admission to the gardens and museums is free between 10am and 1pm on Sundays.

▶ For more insight, join an hour-long guided tour of the exhibition (4pm on Saturdays in English), free with admission to the museum.

✕ Take a Break

Overlooking the park, **Serralves Restaurant** (☎226 170 355; Rua Dom João de Castro 21; lunch buffet €13; ⊙noon-7pm Mon-Fri, 10am-7pm Sat, 10am-8pm Sun) rustles up a pretty good lunch buffet, with soup, salads, vegetarian options and desserts.

The Best of
Porto

Historic houses, central Porto
AROXO/GETTY IMAGES ©

Best Walks
Porto's Unesco World Heritage Heart

🏃 The Walk

Rising in a helter-skelter of chalk-bright houses, soaring bell towers and Gothic and baroque churches, Porto's Unesco-listed historic heart is an alley-woven dream of medieval loveliness made for strolling. Cobblestone streets twist past old curiosity shops and pavement cafes that hum with local gossip, and every so often the cityscape cracks open to reveal *miradouros* (viewpoints) over Porto.

Start Igreja da Misericórdia; Ⓜ São Bento (yellow line)

Finish Ponte de Dom Luís I; Jardim do Morro cable car station

Length 4km; four hours

✕ Take a Break

Pause for lunch near the river. For Douro views, try to snag a terrace table at Bacalhau (p35), where the namesake codfish is the menu star. A Grade (p36) dishes up Portuguese home cooking with a smile.

RIKAMEN/GETTY IMAGES ©

Sé cathedral

❶ Igreja da Misericórdia

Duck down Rua das Flores, one of Ribeira's most charming streets, lined with delis, cafes, boutiques and speciality shops, and splashed with vibrant street art. To the right near the bottom sits the **Igreja da Misericórdia** (p32), a baroque beauty designed by Nicolau Nasoni, with an interior replete with blue and white *azulejos* (hand-painted tiles).

❷ Palácio da Bolsa

A mosey down Rua Ferreira Borges brings you to the Jardim do Infante D Henrique, flanked by the late 19th-century Mercado Ferreira Borges market hall and the neoclassical grandeur of the **Palácio da Bolsa** (p28). Henry the Navigator stands high on a pedestal at the centre of the square.

❸ Igreja de São Francisco

Swinging a right brings you to the Praça Infante Dom Henrique and the **Igreja de São Francisco** (p26), Porto's most sublime church – Gothic on the outside and a feast of over-the-top, gilded baroque splendour on the inside.

❹ Cais da Ribeira

Strolling along **Cais da Ribeira** (p32) is your golden ticket to the city's soul. This is Porto of a million postcards – the Ribeira's chalk-hued houses rising behind you, the Rio Douro unfurling before you, street entertainers serenading you. Colourful *barcos rabelos* (flat-bottomed boats) bob in front of pavement cafes and restaurants and the graceful swoop of the Ponte de Dom Luís I frames the picture neatly.

❺ Sé

Take a steep flight of steps uphill from the river to Porto's crowning glory, the fortress-like **cathedral** (p24). History reverberates in its Romanesque-meets-baroque nave and cloister, and the terrace commands photogenic views of the cityscape.

❻ Ponte de Dom Luís I

Exit right onto Calçada de Vandoma, then veer right again onto Avenida Vimara Peres, which will bring you to that whopper of a double-decker arched bridge, the **Ponte de Dom Luís I** (p32), taking a spectacular leap over the Douro. Cross it for swoonworthy views, keeping your eye out for daredevils jumping off its lower level.

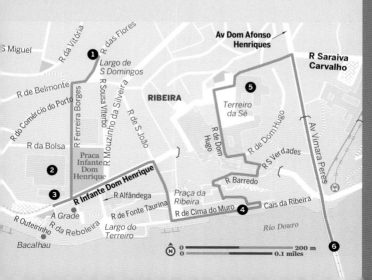

Best Walks
Aliados & Bolhão

🏃 The Walk

Allow at least half a day for this walk from Porto's monumental Avenida dos Aliados to the captivating Igreja do Carmo. En route you'll take in the banter of one of the city's best food markets, old-school, grocery stores, exquisite baroque and Gothic churches, a tower with a view and the magical bookshop that continues to put the Harry Potter in Porto.

Start Avenida dos Aliados; Ⓜ São Bento

Finish Igreja do Carmo; Ⓜ São Bento or Aliados

Length 3km; 3½ hours

✖ Take a Break

Pull up a chair under the gilded woodwork, cherubs and grand mirrors at Café Majestic (p52), a genteel time warp of a cafe and one of JK Rowling's old haunts. Or get juiced and dig into fresh wraps, salads and lunch specials between sights at Liquid (p56).

Igreja do Carmo

❶ Avenida dos Aliados

Paris has the Champs-Élysées and Porto has the **Avenida dos Aliados** (p48), a stately boulevard built high and mighty from pale marble and granite, with all the beaux-arts trimmings. Its centrepiece, *câmara municipal* (town hall), is topped by a 70m tower.

❷ Mercado do Bolhão

Turn right onto Rua Formosa to reach the 19th-century, wrought-iron **Mercado do Bolhão** (p61), a tantalising slice of local life full of foodie treats such as fresh-from-the-Atlantic fish, and wine and cheese stalls.

❸ Capela das Almas

On the pedestrian-only Rua de Santa Catarina, thronged with shoppers, your gaze will be drawn to the 18th-century **Capela das Almas** (p49), with blue and white *azulejo* friezes dancing flamboyantly across its facade.

ALAN COPSON/GETTY IMAGES ©

④ Praça da Batalha

Wander south to Praça da Batalha, a grand plaza home to the splendidly tiled baroque **Igreja de Santo Ildefonso** (p50). Across the way the **Teatro Nacional São João** (p58), the spitting image of Paris' Opéra Garnier in miniature, demands attention.

⑤ Torre dos Clérigos

Amble along Rua de 31 Janeiro and continue along Praça da Liberdade, dominated by an equestrian statue of a dashing King Pedro IV. You'll emerge at Nicolau Nasoni's baroque **tower** (p49). Ascend the 225-step spiral staircase for cracking city views.

⑥ Livraria Lello

Cross Praça de Lisboa and you can't miss this fanciful 1906 neo-Gothic **bookshop** (p59) at the foot of the bar-lined Galeria district. Its bewitching interior with stained-glass skylight and twisting staircase inspired JK Rowling's Harry Potter books during her stint living in Porto.

⑦ Igreja do Carmo

It's just a two-minute toddle from here to the rococo **Igreja do Carmo** (p48), one side of which is clad top to toe in stunning *azulejos* that depict the founding of the Carmelite order.

Best
Eating

With the Atlantic splashing the city's western fringes, the Douro vineyards on the doorstep and the high dairy country of the Trás-os-Montes rolling out east, Porto has rich culinary pickings. Chefs make the most of this bountiful natural larder, and whether it's served in *tascas* (taverns) with a dollop of old-school charm, in boho-flavoured tapas bars or in high-class restaurants with twinkling city views, seasonality, stunning freshness and pride in local sourcing are key.

Take it Slow

Nose-to-tail, farm-to-plate dining is the word in Porto at the moment, where kitchens are increasingly moving in the slow-food lane. Organic produce from small local producers is making its way onto plates in a growing crop of hip and wholesome delis and cafes (some vegetarian and vegan), with rustic-chic decor and a nicely laid-back vibe. *Petiscos* (tapas) – sometimes served with a pinch of imagination – are big, too, slotting in well with Porto's sociable, sharing vibe.

Porto Soul Food

Porto is liberally sprinkled with family-run *tascas* and *tabernas*, no-frills, cheap-as-chips places filled with cheek-by-jowl-tables and local chatter. At some, you'll still get change from a €10 note at lunchtime. Here classics have never gone out of fashion – the *francesinha* (a gut-busting monster of a roast meat, cheese-and-egg-topped sandwich), or *tripas à moda do Porto* (hearty offal and white bean stew), for instance.

☑ **Top Tips**

▶ Save by eating your main meal at lunchtime. The *menu do dia* (fixed menu) or *prato do dia* (day special) is always a good-value option.

▶ The *couvert* (bread, olives, pâté etc) brought to the table as an appetiser costs. Pay for what you eat or feel free to send it away.

▶ Want more of an insight into Porto's food scene? Hook onto an indulgent half-day tour with Taste Porto Food Tours (p51).

Gourmet Heaven

Sparky chefs have put Porto on the gastro map of late, with new-wave takes on the classics that play up ultra-fresh ingredients and robust flavours. Names like Pedro Lemos and Ricardo Costa (The Yeatman) have put the city on the Michelin map, while Rui Paula pairs show-stopping architecture with menus extolling the virtues of Portuguese produce. José Avillez recently rocked up in Porto with a new retro-cool bistro where menus sing of the seasons.

Best Bistros & Delis

Mercearia das Flores Organic, regional grub and pavement seating at this deli delight. (p34)

Casa de Pasto da Palmeira Waterfront charmer with creative dishes made for sharing. (p117)

Papavinhos Delightful family-run number with river views and spot-on Portuguese faves. (p103)

Flor dos Congregados Blackboard specials big on seasonal flavour in a warm, convivial tavern. (p51)

Best Tapas & Tascas

Cantina 32 Industro-retro haunt with charm and imaginative, mouth-watering *petiscos* (tapas). (p36)

Casinha São João Gorgeous river views and great sharing plates. (p35)

Bacalhau Dreamy river views, *petiscos* and novel takes on *bacalhau* (dried salt-cod). (p124)

Taberna São Pedro Breezy, briny, salt-of-the-earth tavern praised far and wide for its fish. (p93)

Taberna do Largo Grocery store, deli and tavern with hand-picked wines and carefully sourced *petiscos*. (p35)

Taberna d'Ávo All stone walls, soft light and moreish *petiscos*. (p76)

Taberna de Santo António Good old-fashioned, no-frills, family-run tavern. (p69)

Best for Romance

O Paparico Romance wrapped in stone-walled, wood-beamed rusticity and food to rave about. (p54)

Ode Porto Wine House Slow food in a beamed, softly lit, delightfully intimate setting. (p37)

O Comercial Dress up for dinner in palatial, chandelier-lit finery. (p36)

Em Carne Viva Romance by day in this cafe with a stuccoed parlour and secret garden. (p110)

Best Gourmet

Cantinho do Avillez Star chef José Avillez elevates seasonal ingredients creatively at this retro-slick bistro. (p35)

DOP Sylish setting and punchy fusion food with Rui Paula at the helm. (p36)

The Yeatman Impecca-ble food and wine with a Michelin star and stellar city views. (p88)

Boa Nova Tea House Álvaro Siza Vieira's aesthetics meet Rui Paula's culinary prow-ess. (p118)

Pedro Lemos Michelin-starred heavyweight, bursting with seasonal flavour. (p118)

Best
Nightlife & Entertainment

While Porto isn't going to steal the clubbing crown any time soon, this high-spirited city still gets its groove on with the best of them until the morning coffee starts to bubble. With just enough grit and urban edge to keep the scene fresh-faced, a night out here can swing from retro bars spinning techno to glam rooftop lounges with cocktails and shimmering city views. With an open mind and a sociable attitude, you'll soon tune into Porto's party-loving soul.

Nightlife Districts

As day fades into watercolour dusk and the river starts to glitter, toast your night in a beachfront haunt in Foz or a river-view bar in Ribeira or Vila Nova de Gaia. The backstreets of Ribeira brim with wine bars ideal for imbibing and conversing. Order a glass of beefy Douro red or sip at an aperitif – a zingy favourite is *porto tónico* (white port and tonic on ice).

As the night wears on, there's only one word on the lips of local ravers: Galerias. The secret in these bar-rammed streets is to go with the flow – drifting from one bar to the next as the mood and music takes you, and sharing laughs with total strangers as the party spills out onto the street.

☑ Top Tips

▶ In typical southern style, nights begin late here. Bars don't really crank up until around 11pm and clubs take over when they close at 2am-ish.

▶ Book concert and theatre tickets at least a week ahead to ensure decent seats.

Best Bars & Late-Night Cafes

Casa do Livro Bookish glamour, DJ beats and a boho vibe. (p45)

Moustache Mellow but cool hang-out with a cultural slant. (p56)

Galeria de Paris Very vintage hipster honeypot that knows how to party. (p45)

Era Uma Vez No Paris A drop of bordello-chic Parisian glamour in Porto. (p45)

Café au Lait DJs rock this former textile warehouse turned intimate bar. (p45)

Café Candelabro Bookstore goes boho bar. (p54)

Gin House Gin, glorious gin. (p45)

Best Wine & Port Bars

Vinologia Snug wine bar with 200 kinds of port to sample. (p37)

Prova Meet Diogo and linger over a tasting of the Douro's finest. (p38)

Wine Quay Bar Prime raise-a-glass sunset material at this riverside number. (p38)

The Wine Box Slick, modern wine bar with tapas. (p38)

Best Roof Terraces & Beach Bars

360º Terrace Lounge River-gazing terrace perched above Vila Nova de Gaia. (p88)

Dick's Bar Sophisticated pick with one of the best cellars (and views) in town. (p90)

Zenith Lounge Bar Porto shrinks from this swanky, 15th-floor lounge. (p113)

Praia da Luz A firm Foz favourite for watching the sun fizz into the Atlantic. (p118)

Best Live Music

Casa da Música The star on Porto's music scene, with first-rate classical and jazz concerts. (p115)

Hot Five Jazz & Blues Club Does what it says on the tin – hot jazz and blues. (p40)

Armazém do Chá DJs and concerts in a former roasting warehouse. (p58)

Breyner 85 This funky townhouse rocks to jam sessions, DJ beats, karaoke and more. (p77)

Fado in Porto If you want to hear the soulful crooning of a *fadista* in Porto, head here. (p90)

Best Clubs

Hard Club Industro-cool club in a 19th-century market hall, with a playlist skipping from hip hop to hard rock. (p40)

Indústria Basement club throbbing to deep house. (p119)

Best Culture & Concerts

Maus Hábitos The darling of Porto's alternative scene, with a varied cultural line-up. (p58)

Teatro Nacional São João Porto's foremost performing arts venue. (p58)

Coliseu do Porto Big-name gigs, theatre and dance. (p58)

Pinguim Café Boho bar with artsy vibe and line-up of plays, film screenings, readings and exhibitions. (p77)

Best
For Kids

Exploring Porto with tots (or teenagers) can be child's play with a little know-how. What could be more kid-friendly, after all, than screeching through the streets on a vintage tram, devising your very own Harry Potter trail in the city that once inspired JK Rowling's magical pen, hitting the beaches in Foz, or finding adventure in the footsteps of great Portuguese navigators?

Happy Families

Porto is inexpensive at the best of times, but it offers cracking value for families. Museums offer free or discounted entry (up to 50%) for under-14s or under-18s, and travel for tots under four is free on public transport. Hotels are often geared up for families and many will squeeze in a cot for no extra charge. All but the poshest restaurants welcome children, appealing to little appetites with either a kids' menu or a *meia dose* (half portion).

Hotels and guesthouses should be able to advise on babysitters and point you in the direction of the nearest pharmacy or supermarket where you can stock up on nappies (diapers) and formula. Pick up the handy *A Visit to Porto* map at the tourist office.

☑ **Top Tips**

▶ Kids under four travel free on public transport.

▶ Museums are free or discounted for under-14s or under-18s.

Boats on the Rio Douro

Best Hands-On Fun

Sealife Porto Kids can watch sharks glide overhead, handle starfish and find Nemo at this whopper of an aquarium. (p117)

Museu das Marionetas Puppets on strings are in the spotlight at this marionette museum. (p34)

World of Discoveries Slip into the shoes of a swashbuckling explorer at this discovery-focused sight. (p101)

Best Art & Inspiration

Serralves Check out the activity-driven family weekend programs at Serralves. (p120)

Ponte de Dom Luís I Budding photographers can practise snapping Porto's simply ginormous bridge. (p32)

Rua das Flores Why not give them a scrapbook and pencils for a self-guided street art tour? (p57)

Best Outdoors

Foz do Douro Hop aboard tram 1 to Foz for ice cream, lighthouse snapshots, beach fun and a paddle in the Atlantic. (p116)

Jardim do Palácio de Cristal Porto is reduced to pop-up-book scale from these glorious gardens complete with peacocks. (p96)

Parque da Cidade Kids love letting off steam in Porto's biggest park. Perfect picnic territory. (p117)

Best
Shopping

Shopping in Porto is very much a local experience, whether you're nosing around fresh produce markets as the city starts to wake up or tasting port before selecting the perfect take-home bottle. Go to gallery-lined Rua Miguel Bombarda for one-of-a-kind art, accessories and fashion by emerging designers, rewind time poking around Aliados backstreets for vintage and vinyl, or visit Bolhão for delightfully old-school grocery stores.

KEVIN GEORGE/ALAMY ©

Best Food

Chocolateria Ecuador Divine dark chocolate bars, pralines and bonbons – all beautifully packaged. (p40)

Central Conserveira da Invicta An Atlantic feast of tinned fish in retro-cool wrappings. (p60)

Garrafeira do Carmo Savvy staff give you the inside scoop on port and Douro wines here. (p79)

A Pérola Do Bolhão Deli heaven with edible delights from mountain cheese and smoky *chouriço* (sausage) to wine and dried fruits. (p60)

Best Art & Design

Galeria São Mamede Plug into Porto's contemporary art scene at this Rua Miguel Bombarda gallery. (p98)

CC Bombarda Mall packed with independent boutiques, from one-off illustrations to urban wear and locally designed accessories. (p99)

CRU Showcase for the one-off work of Portuguese creatives. (p78)

Best Fashion & Vintage

Nuno Balthazar Flagship Porto store of Portugal's catwalk king. (p115)

Flapper Vintage gladrags and glitzy knick-knacks. (p99)

Goodvibes Urban streetwear and funky accessories at this boutique, gallery and concept store. (p60)

La Petite Coquette Girly boudoir of a boutique, crammed with second-hand designer labels. (p61)

Cocktail Molotof Hipster honeypot for bright, show-stopping fashion and accessories. (p99)

Best Crafts & Gifts

A Vida Portuguesa A walk down memory lane with vintage gifts in an old fabric shop. (p59)

Tradições Real Portuguese products, from Alentejo cork designs to Lazuli *azulejos* (hand-painted tiles). (p40)

Lobo Taste Ceramic, wicker and papier-mâché crafts and standout sun hats. (p41)

Prometeu Artesano We dig the quirky mini *azulejo* rings. (p41)

Best
Festivals & Events

Let's face it: the *tripeiros* need little excuse for a party, whether they are whacking each other with squeaky hammers at the riotous Festa de São João, celebrating São Pedro da Afurada by scoffing sardines, drinking *vinho* and dancing till dawn, or bopping to rock at open-air festivals in the sweet nights of summer. The more the merrier is the attitude in this high-spirited city.

Best Cultural & Heritage Events

Serralves Em Festa (www.serralvesemfesta.com) Runs for 40 hours non-stop over one weekend in early June. Parque de Serralves hosts the main events, with concerts, avant-garde theatre and kiddie activities.

Festival Internacional de Teatro de Expressão Ibérica (www.fantasporto. com) Two weeks of contemporary theatre in Spanish and Portuguese; held in late May/early June.

Fantasporto (www.fitei. com) Two weeks of fantasy, horror and just plain weird films in February/ March.

Best Music Festivals

Festival Internacional de Folclore de Gulpilhares A week-long festival in late July/early August; attracts international groups.

Marés Vivas (www.mares vivas.meo.pt.com) Over a weekend in mid-July, Afurada welcomes big rock and pop names to the stage.

Noites Ritual Rock (http://www.porto-tourism. com/porto-events/noites -ritual.html) A weekend-long rock extravaganza in late August.

☑ Top Tips

▶ Porto's wildest all-singing, all-dancing shindigs revolve around the celebration of the Santos Populares Popular Saints) in June.

▶ Join in the head-hammering midsummer madness at Porto's biggest bash, the Festa de São João (Festival of St John; p39) on 23 and 24 June.

▶ Afurada reels in the crowds with fishermen parades, parties and sardine feasting at Festa de São Pedro da Afurada (p90) around 29 June.

Best
Port Wine

The soothing glug-glug of port being poured is music to local ears. And you can't say you've been to Porto until you've tasted the Douro's oak-barrel-aged nectar and learned to tell a mellow, nutty tawny from a complex, sophisticated vintage. Ever since 17th-century British merchants rocked up here in the 17th century, the swanky lodges spilling down Vila Nova de Gaia's hillside have been the nerve centre of port production – they still are today.

ABEL LEÃO/GETTY IMAGES ©

Best for Tasting & Shopping

ViniPortugal Not just port but also Portuguese wine can be tasted at ViniPortugal in the Palácio da Bolsa. (p38)

Prova Diogo is a mine of knowledge about Douro wines and ports. Taste them here by the glass. (p38)

Vinologia Wine bar snuggled away in the historic centre, with 200 ports for the tasting. (p37)

Garrafeira Do Carmo Take your pick from a mind-boggling array of ports at this central store. (p79)

Best Cellar Tours

Taylor's Runs highly informative cellar tours followed by tastings of some of Porto's absolute finest. (p84)

Graham's Perched high above the Douro, this lodge offers great insight into port production, with a three-wine tasting. (p84)

Cálem Award-winning cellars with guided tours and tastings. (p84)

Ramos Pinto Down by the river, with cellars, tours and tastings. (p85)

Croft Going strong since 1588, this rustically elegant lodge carved out of the hillside has tastings. (p85)

Sandeman Guides in black capes lead you through Sandeman's centuries-old cellars. (p85)

Best for Experiencing

Douro Azul Drift along the Douro in replica *barcos rabelos*, flat-bottomed boats that once transported wine from the vineyards. (p34)

Espaço Porto Cruz A contemporary ode to port wine in a historic building, with a museum, restaurant, tastings and terrace. (p83)

Best
For Free

There's so much to discover in Porto without spending a cent. Sunset city views from hilltop *miradouros*, botanical garden strolls, swims in the nearby Atlantic and walks in the alley-woven historic centre, peeling back the layers of history – all free, free and free again. You can see everything from cutting-edge photography to baroque churches smothered in *azulejos* gratis in this astonishingly good-value city.

Weekend Cent Savers

With a little careful timing, you can considerably slash the costs of exploring Porto. Save sightseeing for the weekend. Even big-hitter museums like the art-crammed **Museu Nacional Soares dos Reis** and the cutting-edge **Serralves** open their doors for free on Sunday mornings. And it costs nothing to visit the riverside **Museu do Vinho do Porto**, for an insight into port-wine making, or the charmingly **Museu Romântico**, for a flashback to a more romantic era, at weekends. If you don't have the cash to fork out on tours, plan your own with our inside scoop on local life – from architecture to street art – and 'best of' walk (see p64, p101 and p97.

Best Free Sights

Livraria Lello This neo-Gothic wonder with a pinch of Potter is one of the world's loveliest bookshops. (p59)

São Bento Train Station Rewind back to rail travel's glory days and bone up on Portuguese history admiring *azulejos*. (p48)

MAREMAGNUM/GETTY IMAGES ©

Centro Português de Fotografia Zoom in on cutting-edge photography at this former prison. (p66)

Best Free Outdoors

Jardim do Palácio de Cristal Porto looks toytown tiny framed between towering palms at this botanical beauty. (p96)

Ponte de Dom Luís I Walk the upper level of this double-decker bridge for knockout views, emerging at the Jardim do Morro. (p32)

Foz do Douro Explore a fort, stroll a seafront promenade and paddle in the Atlantic. (p116)

Best
Tours

Best Bus & Tuk-Tuk Tours

Douro Azul Offer cruises in the colourful boats that were once used to transport port wine from the vineyards. (p34)

Tuk Tour (www.tuktour porto.com; Rua das Carmelitas 136) These electric numbers are an eco-cool way to buzz around the city as your clued-up guide shares anecdotes.

Best Walking & Bike Tours

Porto Tours (www.porto tours.com; Torre Medieval, Calçada Pedro Pitões 15) Excellent municipal service provides details of all the recommended tour operators, from city walking tours to helicopter rides over the city.

Blue Dragon Tours (www.bluedragon.pt; Avenida Gustavo Eiffel 280) Runs classic three-hour bike tours and several half-day walking tours.

The Other Side (www. theotherside.pt; Rua Souto 67) Well-informed, congenial guides reveal their city on half-day walking tours of hidden Porto.

Wild Walkers (www. wildwalkerstours.com; Avenida dos Aliados, Praça da Liberdade) Peppered with anecdotes and personality, these young and fun guided walking tours are a great intro to Porto.

Best Themed Tours

We Hate Tourism Tours (www.wehatetourismtours. com/oporto) If you want to sidestep tourist traps and beeline the city's soul, WHTT is the real deal.

Living Tours (www. livingtours.pt; Rua Mouzinho da Silveira 352-4) A great range of sightseeing options are on offer at this friendly agency, from city tours to day trips.

The Worst Tours (www. theworsttours.weebly.com)

KEN WELSH/GETTY IMAGES ©

☑ **Top Tips**

▶ Nibble your way around Porto on a half-day ramble through Aliados and Bolhão with the the brilliant Taste Porto Food Tours (p51).

▶ A novel way to see the city is from behind the wheel of a Renault Twizy on an efun GPS tour (p85).

A trio of out-of-work architects got together to offer free and fun offbeat tours of Porto on foot, each with a different theme.

Best **Outdoors**

Whether it is the enticing sparkle of the river glimpsed wistfully from perkily perched *miradouros* (viewpoints), a sunset snapshot of the city as seen from a lush botanical garden, or a reviving walk or bike ride along the seafront or through the city's biggest park, Porto effortlessly combines the urban with the outdoors. And the heart of Douro wine country is also on the city's doorstep.

PETER ALIX/AGE FOTOSTOCK ©

Lure of the Atlantic

You need only peer up at seagulls wheeling overhead in a crystal-clear blue sky, sample the freshness of the just-caught fish in Afurada, or take on a tram along the ever-broadening river west to sense just how close Porto is to the Atlantic. Why are the *tripeiros* so incredibly laid-back? Well, proximity to the beach certainly helps. Foz do Douro's seafront promenade and sprinkling of beaches are just a short hop from the centre, so you can easily tie in a morning's sightseeing with an afternoon spent licking ice-cream and paddling in the ocean. Even better beaches lie further north in Vila do Conde, an hour's trundle away on the B (red) metro line.

Best Parks

Parque da Cidade Porto's urban escape vault is this mammoth lake-dotted park, complete with cycling and walking trails. (p117)

Jardim da Cordoaria Find leafy respite in this sculpture-strewn park. (p72)

Jardim do Passeio Alegre Breathe in the briny Atlantic air as you saunter through these graceful 19th-century gardens. (p117)

Best Botanical Gardens

Jardim do Palácio de Cristal Secret gardens, flowery parterres, pockets of woodland and drop-dead-gorgeous city views await here. (p96)

Jardim Botânico do Porto Green-fingered students tend these romantic and secluded botanical gardens. (p109)

Best Viewpoints

Miradouro da Vitória See Porto unfurl scenically before you from this Jewish-quarter *miradouro*. (p72)

Jardim do Morro Slung high above the city in Gaia, these pretty gardens command stellar views of the historic centre. (p83)

Jardim das Virtudes Sloping lawns ideal for picnicking and river gazing. (p72)

Best
Churches, Towers & Forts

Romanesque and Gothic, Renaissance and rococo, austere and exuberant – you can map out Porto's past in the profusion of churches scattered across the city, with their mighty towers and spires encrusting Porto's skyline. History seeps through their vaulted naves, *azulejo*-clad cloisters and eerily atmospheric catacombs.

BRENT WINEBRENNER/GETTY IMAGES ©

Best for Views

Sé Porto's crowning glory cathedral is a fortified Romanesque giant with sweeping city views. (p24)

Torre dos Clérigos Porto spreads at your feet from Nicolau Nasoni's 76m-high tower, abutting a church of the same name. (p49)

Forte de São Francisco Xavier The crashing Atlantic is the backbeat at this defensive fort, also known as the Castelo do Queijo (Cheese Castle). (p117)

Mosteiro da Serra de Pilar Rising high and mighty above the river, this 17th-century monastery has a striking central cloister. (p83)

Best Baroque

Igreja de São Francisco Gothic on the outside and a jewel-box of gilded baroque splendour on the inside. (p26)

Igreja de São Pedro de Miragaia A medieval-rooted church with a medieval makeover. (p73)

Igreja Nossa Senhora da Vitória Tucked away in Porto's former Jewish quarter, with an altar sculpture by Soares dos Reis. (p72)

Igreja de Santa Clara Once a Franciscan convent, now a baroque stunner replete with intricate gilded woodwork. (p33)

Best for Azulejos

Igreja da Misericórdia An ornate Nicolau Nasoni gem smothered in *azulejos*. (p32)

Capela das Almas Extraordinary *azulejo*-adorned church, with panels spelling out the lives of saints. (p49)

Igreja do Carmo Stunning *azulejo*-clad church, with a frieze on the facade paying homage to Nossa Senhora (Our Lady). (p48)

Igreja do Corpo Santo de Massarelos *Azulejos* dance across the facade of this church, which pings you back to the Age of Discovery. (p101)

Best
Art & Architecture

Beyond Porto's alley-woven historic heart, contemporary architects have left their idiosyncratic imprint on crisply minimalist buildings that strike a perfect balance with their often-natural surrounds. Winging the city into the 21st century with their show-stopping designs local Pritzker Prize–winning architects Álvaro Siza Vieira and Eduardo Souto de Moura are the dream duo. Public art from *azulejos* to street art also add an element of interest to the every day.

ALAN COPSON/GETTY IMAGES ©

☑ **Top Tips**

▶ Get inspiration for your own self-guided tour of Porto's hottest contemporary architecture with the free maps guides hand out at the tourist office.

Best Historic Highs

Sé Porto's fortress-like Romanesque cathedral has Gothic and baroque touches. (p24)

São Bento Train Station A romantic, *azulejo*-clad edifice in beaux-arts style. (p48)

Palácio da Bolsa Austerely neoclassical on the outside, Porto's former stock exchange hides exquisite interiors. (p28)

Avenida dos Aliados The grand and the glorious buildings that line this avenue present a roll call of architectural styles – from neoclas-

sical to French beaux-arts. (p48)

Igreja de São Francisco A lavishly gilded baroque treat. (p26)

Best Street Art

Avenida dos Aliados Six telephone boxes funked up by the likes of street artist Costah. (p48)

Rua Miguel Bombarda Gallery dotted and street-art splashed. (p98)

Best Cutting-Edge Architecture

Casa da Música Porto's iconic Rem Koolhaas–designed concert hall

takes acoustics to another dimension. (p106)

Museu de Arte Contemporânea An angular, whitewashed Álvaro Siza Vieira–designed gallery, set in parkland and amplifying light and space. (p121)

Boa Nova Tea House A clifftop stunner overlooking the ocean by starchitect Vieira. (p118)

Best
Museums

Dipping into Porto's museums gives you real insight into how the city has been shaped by the past and precisely what makes it tick today. Some of the museums are small, intimate numbers, homing in on special interests from port wine to puppets, while others are altogether much grander affairs, housed in stately palaces or minimalist buildings on the cutting-edge of cool.

RICHARD CUMMINS/GETTY IMAGES ©

Best Ancient & Contemporary Art

Museu Nacional Soares dos Reis Porto's must-see art museum is a spectacular romp through fine and decorative arts. (p64)

Museu de Arte Contemporânea Engaging exhibitions of contemporary art in a minimalist Álvaro Siza Vieira–designed edifice. (p121)

Centro Português de Fotografia Click into today's photography scene at this born-again prison. (p66)

Best Special Interest

Museu das Marionetas Find out who pulls the strings of the mari-onettes at this family-friendly museum. (p34)

Museu dos Transportes Trace cars, radio and telecom back to their roots in this grand 19th-century customs house. (p73)

Museu do Vinho do Porto Riverside warehouse revamped into a museum showcasing the history of wine- and port-making. (p101)

Museu do Carro Eléctrico Love Porto's vintage trams? This one's for you. (p101)

Best for Heritage

Casa do Infante Age of Discovery superstar, Henry the Navigator, was born in Porto's first customs house in 1394. (p34)

☑ **Top Tips**

▶ Time your visit right. Most museums and sights close on Mondays, and many offer free admission at least one morning at the weekend.

▶ Bear in mind that most museums and sights don't permit photography (at least with a flash). If in doubt, ask first.

Museu Romântico This fine romance of a museum is where the exiled king of Sardinia spent his final days. (p97)

Palácio da Bolsa Porto's opulent Stock Exchange Palace reveals the dazzling wealth of the city's former moneybags. (p28)

Survival Guide

Survival Guide

Before You Go

When to Go

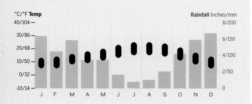

°C/°F **Temp**
40/104 —
30/86 —
20/68 —
10/50 —
0/32 —
-10/14 —

Rainfall Inches/mm
8/200
6/150
4/100
2/50
0

J F M A M J J A S O N D

➡ **Winter** (Nov–Feb)
Quiet but for the Porto marathon in November and São Silvestre race (1 December). Weather can be wet. Accommodation bargains abound.

➡ **Spring** (Mar–May)
Mild temps, gardens in bloom and reasonable room rates. Fantasy film fest in early March.

➡ **Summer** (Jun–Aug)
Peak season for open-air festivals, beach days and alfresco dining. Beds are at a premium during the Festa de São João in June.

➡ **Autumn** (Sep & Oct)
Few crowds and usually warm, though expect the odd shower.

Book Your Stay

Useful Websites

Go2:oporto (www.go2 oporto.com) Good selection of central apartment rentals, with rates starting at around €50 per night.

Lonely Planet (www.lonely planet.com/hotels) Author-recommended reviews and online booking.

Oporto City Center Apartments (www.oporto citycenterapartments.com) Modern, well-equipped studios and apartments in the historic centre.

GoOporto (www.gooporto. com/porto-apartments) Central apartment rentals for up to six people.

Flat in Porto (www.flatin porto.com) Short-term rentals in Porto, starting from three-night stays.

Best Budget

Tattva Design Hostel
(www.tattvadesignhostel.
com) Backpacker heaven
with superb facilities,
attractive rooms and an
open-air rooftop lounge.

Magnólia Hostel (www.
magnoliaporto.com) Well-
maintained hostel in a
converted townhouse,
with a lounge, leafy
outdoor space and free
walking tours.

Gallery Hostel (www.
gallery-hostel.com) A hostel-
gallery with a sunny,
glass-enclosed back pa-
tio, terrace, cinema room
and shared kitchen.

B&B Hotel Porto (www.
hotelbb.pt) Stylish, central
number set in a restored
art-deco building (and
former cinema).

Dixo's Oporto Hostel
(www.dixosoportohostel.com)
Cool, colourful hostel
on the first-floor of a
townhouse, just up from
Ribeira.

Poets Inn (www.oporto
poetshostel.com) Laid-back
B&B in a central but
tucked-away location,
with doubles decorated
by local artists, a garden
and a guest kitchen.

Best Midrange

6 Only (www.6only.pt)
Beautifully restored
guesthouse with just six
rooms, a lounge and a
Zen-like courtyard.

ROSA ET AL (www.
rosaetal.pt) Gorgeous
townhouse in the thick of
Porto's art district, with
six suites, a great restaurant and a lovely garden
out back.

Pensão Favorita (www.
pensaofavorita.pt) An artful
addition to Porto, with
inviting rooms, a lounge
and a restaurant with
outdoor seating.

Castelo Santa Catarina
(www.castelosantacatarina
.com.pt) Whimsical,
pseudo-Gothic castle
with elegant, period-
furnished doubles and
palm-shaded gardens.

**Hotel Eurostars das
Artes** (www.eurostars
hotels.com) Stylish, central
hotel with handsomely
outfitted rooms.

Best Top End

4Rooms (www.4rooms.
pt) Stunningly converted
19th-century townhouse
in Foz redesigned by
prize-winning architect
Eduardo Souto de Moura.

The Yeatman (www.
the-yeatman-hotel.com)
Classy five-star resort
with dazzling city views,
a spa, Michelin-starred
restaurant and Taylor's
opposite.

Guest House Douro
(www.guesthousedouro.com)
Eight elegantly furnished
rooms – the best with
Douro views – and impec-
cable service.

Pestana Porto Hotel
(www.pestana.com) Right on
the Douro, this is one of
Porto's most sophisti-
cated sleeps.

Arriving in Porto

☑ **Top Tip** For the best
way to get to your accom-
modation, see p17.

From Porto Airport

➡ **Metro** (www.metrodo
porto.pt) connections
depart every 20 to 30
minutes from 6am to
12.30am, linking the
airport to central Porto.
Take the violet line E
(direction Estádio do
Dragão). The line stops at
Casa da Música (for

Boavista neighbourhood) and Bolhão. Change at Trindade for the yellow line D (direction Santo Ovídio) for Aliados and São Bento; the latter is the closest stop for the Ribeira district. A one-way ticket costs €1.85 and takes about 45 minutes.

→ **STCP** (Sociedade de Transportes Colectivos do Porto; ☎808 200 166; www.stcp. pt) operates a couple of public buses between the

Tickets & Passes

→ The rechargeable **Andante Card** (www.linhandante. com), costing €0.60 and valid for one year, allows smooth movement between metro, funicular, tram and many bus lines. Charge it with the travel credit according to which zones you will be travelling in. You can purchase credit from metro ticket machines.

→ A 24-hour pass covering the entire network (except for trams) costs €7.

airport and the centre; the most useful is the 601 to Cordoaria, departing every 30 minutes from 5.30am to 11.30pm. A single costs €1.85.

→ A daytime taxi to central Porto takes 20 to 30 minutes and will cost between €20 and €30, plus an extra €1.60 for luggage.

From São Bento Train Station

→ Right in the heart of historic Porto, the exquisitely tiled **São Bento Train Station** (Map p46, D5; Praça Almeida Garrett) is the departure point for most *urbano*, *regional* and *interregional* (IR) trains.

→ São Bento is on the yellow D metro line, two stops from Aliados.

→ For train timetables and fares, visit www.cp.pt.

From Campanhã

→ Many inter-regional, international and all intercity services pull in and out of **Campanhã** (☉9am-7pm) train station, 3km east of the centre.

→ Campanhã is connected to the centre by five metro lines. It's four stops from Trindade, where you can change for Aliados and São Bento.

Getting Around

Metro

→ Porto's metro is compact and fairly easy to navigate – though not comprehensive. It comprises six metropolitan lines that all converge at the Trindade stop.

→ Tickets cost €1.20/ 1.50/1.85 for zone 2/3/4 with an Andante Card. Zone 2 covers the whole city centre east to Campanhã train station, south to Vila Nova de Gaia and west to Foz do Douro.

→ Each trip allows you an hour to move between methods of transport without additional cost.

→ Tickets need to be validated before you begin your journey. Wave the card in front of a machine marked 'Andante'.

→ For timetables, fares and maps, visit www. metrodoporto.pt.

→ The metro runs from around 6am to 1am daily.

Tram, Bus & Funicular

→ Porto's public transport system is operated by **STCP** (www.stcp.pt).

Visit the website for timetables, fares, maps and a journey planner.

➡ Central hubs of Porto's extensive bus system include Jardim da Cordoaria, Praça da Liberdade and São Bento station. Tickets are purchased on the bus; one-way €1.20 with the Andante Card.

➡ The panoramic **Funicular dos Guindais** (one way €2; ⏰8am-10pm, shorter hours in winter) shuttles up and down a steep incline from Avenida Gustavo Eiffel to Rua Augusto Rosa.

➡ Three antique trams trundle around town from roughly 9.30am to 9pm (shorter hours in winter). The most useful line, 1E, travels along the Douro towards the Foz district. One-way tickets cost €2.50, a day pass €8.

➡ The gondola sweeps up from the riverfront in Vila Nova de Gaia to Serra do Pilar, providing scenic views of the centre.

Bicycle

➡ Porto's hilly backstreets require a lot of pedal power, but cycling along the Rio Douro, for instance from Vila Nova de Gaia to Massarelos, or from Ribeira to Foz do Douro, is easier going.

➡ See the Explore chapters for rent-a-bike outlets, or try **Fold 'n' Visit** (☎220 997 106; www. foldnvisit.com; Rua Alferes Malheiro 139; bike rental half/ full day from €13/17) near Trindade metro station, which offers bike rentals and upbeat city tours – a three-hour spin of Porto downtown for €17 to €29 per person, depending on group numbers.

Taxi

➡ To cross town, expect to pay between €5 and €8. There's a 20% surcharge at night, and an additional charge to leave city limits, which includes Vila Nova de Gaia. There are taxi ranks throughout the centre or you can call a taxi.

➡ For a taxi, try **Táxis Invicta** (☎225 076 400)

Essential Information

☑ **Top Tip** Many shops close on Sunday and some shut early Saturday. Small boutiques may close for lunch (1pm to 3pm). Monday is the day off for most museums.

Business Hours

Exceptions to the following are noted in listings:

Restaurants noon-3pm & 7-10pm

Bars 7pm-2am

Cafes 9am-midnight

Clubs 11pm-6am Thu-Sat

Shops 10am-7pm Mon-Sat

Banks 8.30am-3pm Mon-Fri

Post offices 9am-6pm Mon-Fri

Discount Cards

If you plan on doing a lot of sightseeing, it's worth investing in the **Porto Card**, which gives you entry to 11 museums (and a 50% discount on eight others), plus discounts on Douro cruises, tours, visits to the wine cellars, bike rental and car hire. You'll also get reductions at certain restaurants, shops and bars. More expensive versions of the card include public transport; the metro, city buses and CP Porto urban trains. Validate your card before use.The card is available at all **Turismo do Porto** (www.visitporto.travel) tourist offices, including the one at the airport, and São Bento and Campanhã train stations. A one/two/

three-day pass including public transport costs €10.50/17.50/21.50. A two-/three-day walker pass costs €8/10.

Electricity

230V/50Hz

120V/60Hz

Emergency

Police ☏112
Fire ☏112
Ambulance ☏112

Money

☑ **Top Tip** Bear in mind that some small, family-run shops, guesthouses and restaurants accept cash only – if in doubt, ask first.

➡ The Portuguese currency is the euro (€), divided into 100 cents.

➡ Visa is widely accepted, as is MasterCard; American Express and Diners Card less so, with the exception of top-end hotels and restaurants.

➡ Many automated services, such as ticket machines, require a chip-and-pin credit card.

➡ Most banks have a Multibanco ATM, with menus in English (and other languages). You just need your card and PIN. Your home bank will usually charge around 1% to 2% per transaction.

➡ Banks and *bureaux de change* are free to set their own rates and commissions, so a low commission might mean a skewed exchange rate.

➡ Service is not usually added to the bill. Tip an

average of 10% for good service in restaurants. It's courteous to leave a bit of spare change in bars and cafes. Round up to the nearest euro in taxis.

Public Holidays

Banks, offices, department stores and some shops and restaurants close on public holidays.

New Year's Day 1 January
Carnival Tuesday
February/March – the day before Ash Wednesday
Good Friday March/April
Liberty Day 25 April – celebrating the 1974 revolution
Labour Day 1 May
Corpus Christi May/June – ninth Thursday after Easter
Portugal Day 10 June – also known as Camões and Community Day
Feast of the Assumption 15 August
Republic Day 5 October – commemorating the 1910 declaration of the Portuguese Republic
All Saint's Day 1 November
Independence Day 1 December – commemorating the 1640 restoration of independence from Spain

Feast of the Immaculate Conception 8 December
Christmas Day 25 December

Safe Travel

☑ **Top Tip** Take usual commonsense precautions against pickpockets and bag-snatchers, many of whom operate in rush-hour crowds. Keep values stashed away out of sight.

➡ While Porto is generally quite safe, exercise caution after dark in the alleys of the Ribeira district as well as in the area between the São Bento station and the cathedral.

➡ Before jumping in the sea at Foz do Douro, ask about conditions – pollution has been a problem in the past and doubts have been cast on recent claims of purity. If you have qualms, head to Vila do Conde, 26km north.

➡ There is a multilingual **tourist police** (📞222 081 833; Rua Clube dos Fenianos 1; ⏲8am-2am) station beside the city *turismo*.

Telephone

☑ **Top Tip** Buy a local SIM card to save on roaming charges.

➡ To call Portugal from abroad, dial the international access code (📞00), then Portugal's country code (📞351), then the number. All domestic numbers have nine digits and there are no area codes.

➡ Most public phones only accept cards, which are available at most post offices and newsagents. A few coin-operated phones are still around.

➡ You can also make calls from the public telephone booths at the São Bento train station. Pay when your call is finished.

➡ Long-distance and international calls are cheaper from 9pm to 9am weekdays, all weekend and on holidays.

➡ The directory inquiries number is 📞118. The international directory inquiries number is 📞177.

Toilets

☑ **Top Tip** You'll often find public toilets at train and major metro stations, as well as in department stores and malls.

➡ Public toilets in Porto are few and far between. Your best bet is to nip into the nearest cafe or bar. If you just want to use the loo, order the cheapest thing on the menu – an espresso (*cimbalinho*) usually costs around €0.60.

Tourist Information

Porto's helpful tourist offices offer free city maps and info.

City Centre Turismo (📞223 393 472; www.visit porto.travel; Rua Clube dos Fenianos 25; ⏲9am-8pm high season, 9am-7pm low season) The main *turismo* has a detailed city map, a transport map and cultural calendar. Can assist with room bookings, theatre tickets, tours and more.

iPoint Campanhã (Estação de Comboio de Campanhã; ⏲10am-1.30pm & 2.30-7pm) Seasonal info kiosk run by the *turismo* at the Campanhã train station.

iPoint Ribeira (Praça da Ribeira; ⏲10am-7pm Apr-Oct) Useful *turismo*-run info kiosk on Praça da Ribeira, open seasonally.

Turismo (Sé) (📞223 393 472; Terreiro da Sé; ⏲9am-8pm Jun-Oct, 9am-7pm Nov-May) Handy office right next to the cathedral. Offers a ticket and hotel booking service.

Turismo (Gaia) (📞223 773 088; www.cm-gaia.pt; Av Diogo Leite 242; ⏲10am-6pm Mon-Fri, 10am-1pm & 2-6pm Sat) Has a good town map and a brochure listing all lodges open for tours.

Language

Most sounds in Portuguese are also found in English. The exceptions are the nasal vowels (represented in our pronunciation guides by 'ng' after the vowel), pronounced as if you're trying to make the sound through your nose; and the strongly rolled *r* (represented by 'rr' in our pronunciation guides). Note that the symbol 'zh' sounds like the 's' in 'pleasure'. Keeping these points in mind and reading the pronunciation guides as if they were English, you'll be understood just fine. The stressed syllables are indicated with italics.

To enhance your trip with a phrasebook, visit **lonelyplanet.com**. Lonely Planet iPhone phrasebooks are available through the Apple App store.

Basics

Hello.
Olá.   o·laa

Goodbye.
Adeus.   a·de·oosh

How are you?
Como está?   ko·moo shtaa

Fine, and you?
Bem, e você?   beng e vo·se

Please.
Por favor.   poor fa·vor

Thank you.
Obrigado. (m)   o·bree·gaa·doo
Obrigada. (f)   o·bree·gaa·da

Excuse me.
Faz favor.   faash fa·vor

Sorry.
Desculpe.   desh·kool·pe

Yes./No.
Sim./Não.   seeng/nowng

I don't understand.
Não entendo.   nowng eng·teng·doo

Do you speak English?
Fala inglês?   faa·la eeng·glesh

Eating & Drinking

..., please.
..., por favor.   ... poor fa·vor

A coffee	*Um café*	oong ka·fe
A table for two	*Uma mesa para duas pessoas*	oo·ma me·za pa·ra doo·ash pe·so·ash
Two beers	*Dois cervejas*	doysh ser·ve·zhash

I'm a vegetarian.
Eu sou   e·oo soh
vegetariano/   ve·zhe·a·ree·a·noo/
vegetariana. (m/f)   ve·zhe·a·ree·a·na

Cheers!
Saúde!   sa·oo·de

That was delicious!
Isto estava   eesh·too shtaa·va
delicioso.   de·lee·see·o·zoo

The bill, please.
A conta, por favor.   a kong·ta poor fa·vor

Shopping

I'd like to buy ...
Queria   ke·ree·a
comprar ...   kong·praar ...

I'm just looking.
Estou só a ver.   shtoh so a ver

How much is it?
Quanto custa?   kwang·too koosh·ta

It's too expensive.
Está muito   shtaa mweeng·too
caro.   kaa·roo

Can you lower the price?
Pode baixar   po·de bai·shaar
o preço?   oo pre·soo

Emergencies

Help!
Socorro!   soo·ko·rroo

Call a doctor!
Chame um   shaa·me oong
médico!   me·dee·koo

Call the police!
Chame a   shaa·me a
polícia!   poo·lee·sya

I'm sick.
Estou doente.   shtoh doo·eng·te

I'm lost.
Estou perdido. (m)   shtoh per·dee·doo
Estou perdida. (f)   shtoh per·dee·da

Where's the toilet?
Onde é a casa de   ong·de e a kaa·za de
banho?   ba·nyoo

Time & Numbers

What time is it?
Que horas são?   kee o·rash sowng

It's (10) o'clock.
São (dez) horas.   sowng (desh) o·rash

Half past (10).
(Dez) e meia.   (desh) e may·a

morning   *manhã*   ma·nyang
afternoon   *tarde*   taar·de
evening   *noite*   noy·te

yesterday	*ontem*	ong·teng
today	*hoje*	o·zhe
tomorrow	*amanhã*	aa·ma·nyang

1	*um*	oong
2	*dois*	doysh
3	*três*	tresh
4	*quatro*	kwaa·troo
5	*cinco*	seeng·koo
6	*seis*	saysh
7	*sete*	se·te
8	*oito*	oy·too
9	*nove*	no·ve
10	*dez*	desh

Transport & Directions

Where's ...?
Onde é ...?   ong·de e ...

What's the address?
Qual é o   kwaal e oo
endereço?   eng·de·re·soo

Can you show me (on the map)?
Pode-me   po·de·me
mostrar   moosh·traar
(no mapa)?   (noo maa·pa)

When's the next bus?
Quando é que sai   kwang·doo e ke sai
o próximo   oo pro·see·moo
autocarro?   ow·to·kaa·rroo

I want to go to ...
Queria ir a ...   ke·ree·a eer a ...

Does it stop at ...?
Pára em ...?   paa·ra eng ...

Please stop here.
Por favor pare   poor fa·vor paa·re
aqui.   a·kee

Behind the Scenes

Send Us Your Feedback

We love to hear from travellers – your comments help make our books better. We read every word, and we guarantee that your feedback goes straight to the authors. Visit **lonelyplanet.com/contact** to submit your updates and suggestions.

Note: We may edit, reproduce and incorporate your comments in Lonely Planet products such as guidebooks, websites and digital products, so let us know if you don't want your comments reproduced or your name acknowledged. For a copy of our privacy policy visit lonelyplanet.com/privacy.

Kerry's Thanks

I'd like to say a heartfelt *obrigada* to Porto's incredibly friendly locals who made this guide what it is. Big thanks especially go to gastro guru André Apolinário (Taste Porto Food Tours), port wine whizz Ana Sofia (Taylor's), inside expert André (We Hate Tourism Tours) and Alexandra Santos (Porto Convention & Visitors Bureau).

Acknowledgments

Cover photograph: Port wine ships at Vila Nova de Gaia; Cro Magnon/ Alamy.

This Book

This 1st edition of Lonely Planet's *Pocket Porto* was researched and written by Kerry Christiani. This guidebook was produced by the following:

Destination Editors Jo Cooke, Lorna Parkes **Product Editor** Kate James **Coordinating Editor** Carly Hall **Senior Cartographer** Anthony Phelan **Book Designer** Wibowo

Rusli **Assisting Editor** Gabrielle Stefanos **Cover Researcher** Naomi Parker **Thanks to** Karyn Noble, Martine Power, Angela Tinson, Tony Wheeler

Index

Our Writer

Kerry Christiani

Kerry has had a soft spot for Portugal since her first visit here as a child. She jumped at the chance to write about Porto, a city that she loved at first sight with its pristine historic centre, hilltop gardens and atmospheric port lodges – all offering dreamy views over the Douro and out to the Atlantic. For this first edition, she spent a mixed-weather autumn exploring the city's hidden nooks and crannies, getting versed in port wine and eating like a queen in homely *tascas* and backstreet cafes. She studied Portuguese translation to MA level before going on to author more than a dozen Lonely Planet titles, including *Pocket Lisbon*. She tweets @kerrychristiani and lists her work at www.kerrychristiani.com.

Published by Lonely Planet Publications Pty Ltd
ABN 36 005 607 983
1st edition – Sep 2015
ISBN 978 1 74360 595 0
© Lonely Planet 2015 Photographs © as indicated 2015
10 9 8 7 6 5 4 3 2 1
Printed in China